SCHOLAST

Grades

Phonics & Fluency Practice

With Poetry

Lessons That Tap the Power of Rhyming Verse
to Improve Students' Word Recognition, Automaticity,
and Prosody—and Help Them Become Successful Readers

Timothy V. Rasinski,
William H. Rupley, & William Dee Nichols

New York • Toronto • London • Auckland • Sydney
Mexico City • New Delhi • Hong Kong • Buenos Aires

Teaching *Resources*

Dedication

We dedicate this book to all the teachers who see that
teaching reading is an art as well as a science.

TR, WR, WN

"You will not find poetry anywhere unless you bring some of it with you."

—Joseph Joubert

Credits: p. 43: Illustrations © 2011 by Lauren E. Williams. p. 48: "Yankee Doodle on a Chicken" © 2001 by Bruce Lansky. Reprinted from *The Dog Ate My Homework*, with the permission of Meadowbrook Press. p. 48: "Yankee Doodle's Nose Is Running" © 2000 by Bruce Lansky. Reprinted from *If Pigs Could Fly . . . and Other Deep Thoughts*, with the permission of Meadowbrook Press. pp. 48–50: "Wee Willie Winkie," "Wee Willie Stinky," "Another Wee Willie Winkie," "You Are My Teacher," "You Are My Student," "A Test: List of All Fifty States" © TK by Rob Pottle. Used by permission of the author. p. 50: "I'm so Carsick" © 2001 by Alan Katz. From *Take Me Out to the Bathtub*, published by Margaret K. McElderry Books, Simon & Schuster Publishing. p. 53: "Old MacDonald" parody © 2010 by David Harrison. Used by permission of the author.

Cover design: Jorge J. Namerow
Cover photograph: © Tim Pannell/Corbis
Interior design: Sarah Morrow
Development Editor: Joanna Davis-Swing
Editor: Sarah Glasscock

ISBN: 978-0-545-21186-4

Contents

Chapter 1

A Practical Model of Reading

Effective reading instruction means that we need an understanding of what is involved in reading and in learning to read. This chapter describes a simple but valid model of reading and the competencies a student must acquire in order to become a good reader. We also make the case that is the foundation of our book: Poetry, song lyrics, and rhymes are ideal texts for helping students acquire these key reading competencies.

Learning to read and teaching someone to read are incredible accomplishments. When we consider all that is involved in learning to read, it truly borders on the miraculous. Reading involves a thinking mind in understanding language and making meaning; it involves the following: visual perception for intaking printed symbols; the auditory system for turning the written symbols into oral language; the affective and the emotions, as content can trigger a variety of emotional responses. Reading is a social activity promoting engagement through discussing, arguing, questioning, and sharing with one another. It is also a means of enabling us to identify our cultural roots.

Yes, learning to read and the process of reading are truly complex activities. And while most students are successful in acquiring the ability to read, teachers and reading scholars are constantly on the lookout for new and more effective ways to help students acquire this all-important competency.

Since the late 1990s, the field of reading and reading instruction has taken a decidedly scientific focus on how best to teach reading. The National Reading Panel (NRP) (2000) was given the huge task of reviewing existing research on reading and identifying those factors that empirical research could verify as having a positive impact on learning to read. The NRP identified the following five instructional factors that are essential for reading success:

1. phonemic awareness
2. phonics or word decoding
3. vocabulary or word meaning
4. reading fluency
5. comprehension

Most approaches to reading instruction developed since the NRP report have attempted to incorporate these factors into their programs. Our book deals with two specific factors: phonics and fluency. However, we would argue that, in a larger sense, by dealing with phonics and fluency, we are also laying the groundwork for growth in the other factors as well: phonemic awareness, vocabulary, and especially comprehension.

To explain how all these factors are tied together, we would like to begin by sharing a simple model of reading (see Figure 1). Although we acknowledge that this model is certainly not a comprehensive view of reading, we feel it does provide a model for understanding how the various factors involved in reading work together. You will notice that the five factors mentioned earlier are positioned in such a way as to show how they interact with one another.

The horizontal line in the model delineates what the noted linguist Noam Chomsky (1957) identified as the surface structure and deep structure of language. The deep structure is essentially meaning or comprehension, the ultimate goal of reading. Word recognition and fluency are located above the line in what we have termed surface structure. Surface structure refers to the observable part of reading—the print itself. Phonics (and its cousin, phonemic awareness) and fluency are competencies that readers use to make it through the surface structure of reading—to decode the print. We recognize that the surface structure is the least important part of reading. Deep structure is always what we want our students working toward. But here's the problem: In order for readers to dive deep into meaning, they first have to be able to break through the surface. They need to be able to decode words in the text accurately, automatically, and prosodically. Research has shown that most readers who experience difficulty with comprehension exhibit some difficulty in one of the surface-level tasks—phonics and/or

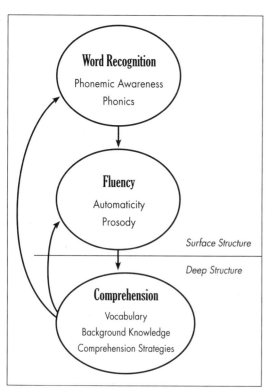

Figure 1: *A Simple Model of Reading*

fluency (Duke, Pressley & Hilden, 2004). As a result of their difficulties in phonics or fluency, comprehension suffers, and they are unable to dive deep into meaning.

As students gain proficiency in phonics and fluency, they are able to break through the surface and use their background knowledge, their knowledge of word meanings, and the various comprehension strategies we teach them to make meaning. As readers continue to read and make meaning, they will be improving their word recognition and fluency competencies, which will lead to even further improvements in comprehension. Once we have moved students to the point where they are able to break through that surface structure and make meaning, the process of reading itself will lead to even greater improvements in all reading competencies.

Our point in presenting this model is to demonstrate to you that, although word decoding and fluent reading are not the ultimate goal of reading, they are essential to allowing readers access to meaning, to making sense of the reading. So in developing this book on the teaching of phonics and fluency, we are also developing a book on comprehension and vocabulary as well. We hope you agree.

Phonics

* *

We want students to be able to turn the written symbols of words into their oral representation. Phonics is one way to make this happen. Phonics is a reading competency that involves learning to use the sound-symbol relationship embedded in written words in order to produce the oral representation of words. English is a sound-based language. Letters (e.g., *s, t, a, m, p*) and letter combinations (*at, ate, ight, tion*) represent sounds and combinations of sounds. Phonics is simply the approach to word decoding that takes advantage of the sound-symbol relationships in written English. And since written English is a sound-based language, it makes good sense to teach word decoding through phonics.

However, it is important to note that there are other ways that readers can develop an oral representation of a printed word. The use of linguistic context is one way. Often a reader can figure out the pronunciation of a word from the meaning that precedes or comes after the unknown word itself. Consider the following sentence: *I was so hungry I jumped in my car and drove to the nearest r_____ .*

Although only the first letter of the last word is presented, you are very likely able to determine the pronunciation of that last word from the meaning that preceded it. When a person is hungry and in a car, they will probably head to a place where they can satisfy their hunger—and if that place begins with the letter *r*, we are almost a hundred percent certain that the word is *restaurant*. Pictures that accompany a written text can also provide clues to the pronunciation of words in the text. However, although linguistic and graphic context are helpful in word decoding, they are not the most efficient way to decode words (Stanovich, 1980; Nicholson, Lillas, & Rzoska, 1988) and can often lead readers astray in guessing the wrong word, which results in missing the message.

Although readers can use context to figure out unknown words, the process of using context requires a considerable amount of cognitive effort, effort that would be better used to make meaning or comprehend what the author is trying to communicate rather than how an individual word might be pronounced. Research has shown that students who struggle in reading are more likely to use context to decode words than more proficient students (Stanovich, 1980; Nicholson, Lillas, & Rzoska, 1988).

Actually, the most efficient way to decode words is the way that most proficient readers decode words—instantly, by knowing the letter combinations and automatically recognizing the word. Most of the words we encounter as adult proficient readers are essentially memorized from previous encounters. We call these words "sight words" because we can recognize or decode them holistically upon seeing them. In reality, proficient readers hardly ever use phonics or context to decode words. They don't need to; think about your own reading. How often do you actually have to stop at a word to sound it out or figure it out from the surrounding meaning? Our guess is that your answer is "hardly ever." Most of the word decoding done by proficient readers involves the instant recognition of words we have seen so many times that they have become embedded in our memory by sight, sound, and meaning.

So why is phonics so important? There are two reasons. One, it is the tool that most readers use for getting words into their memory in the first place. Sight words only become sight words after a reader has seen them repeatedly and developed a sense of orthography. But if a reader has never seen a word before, it cannot be a sight word. So the initial encounter with an unknown word requires a tool for decoding it. Phonics is probably the best way to do that initial decoding. Subsequent encounters with the same word will result in its becoming memorized to the point of sight recognition.

The second reason that phonics is important is that even proficient readers will occasionally come across words that they have never previously encountered. When this happens, they need tools to decode the unfamiliar word. Again, phonics is a very productive tool for this task.

Teaching Phonics

Phonics is one of many ways to decode printed words. Because it is so important, many scholars feel that it should be directly and intensively taught as early as possible in a student's academic life. Proficiency in phonics gives readers the ability to read independently. And once students can read independently, building on this independent reading capability can then help them develop the other reading competencies.

There are many ways of teaching phonics. One approach involves having students infer letter-sound relationships from encountering multiple words that feature a particular phonics element. From repeated encounters with words such as *ball, bat, bear, boy*, and *basket*, students learn that the letter *b* represents the sound /b/. Another approach is to teach children the individual sounds of each letter, as well as the various phonics rules that apply to letter-sound relationships under various conditions (e.g. "when two vowels go walking, the first one does the talking"), and then have them decode words letter by letter, employing their knowledge of rules, letters, and sounds, and then blending the sounds together to make the word. Although both of the above approaches can be successful in teaching phonics to students, we are also advocates of an approach that we call the word family approach to phonics.

Word Families

* *

A word family is a fairly common or frequently occurring combination of letters that have a very consistent sound or combination of sounds associated with them and the words are regular, in that they are spelled the way they sound. More specifically, a word family is the combination of letters in a syllable that begins with the sounded vowel and contains any subsequent letters in the syllable. For example, the following list shows several words and the word families they contain.

bat.........-*at*		western.........-*est*, -*ern*	
spill........-*ill*		butter...........-*ut*, -*er*	
stack.......-*ack*		important.......-*im*, -*or*, -*ant*	
mile........-*ile*		outstanding.....-*out*, -*an*, -*ing*	

As you can see, word families are everywhere. Although we often associate word families with short one-syllable words, knowledge of word families can also help readers decode complex, multisyllabic words.

Word families often go by other names as well, such as *phonograms* and *rimes*. We prefer the

Phonics & Fluency Practice With Poetry © 2012 by Rasinski, Rupley, & Nichols • Scholastic Teaching Resources

term *word families* because it implies a relationship that exists among words that are contained in the same word family. For example, *cat, fat, bat,* and *rat* all belong to the same word family (*-at*). Similarly, *mile, tile, pile, rile, smile,* and *while* also belong to the same word family (*-ile*).

We subscribe to the word family approach to phonics for a number of reasons.

1. First, we recognize the large number of reading and phonics scholars who, based on existing empirical research, recommend the use of word families for teaching phonics (e.g., Adams, 1990; Cunningham, 2004; Fox, 2007; Moustafa, 1997; Rasinski & Padak, 2007; Stahl, 1992).

2. Word families are combinations of letters that are perceived as one unit. It is considerably more efficient to process an unknown word with the fewest number of letter-sound units. For example, the word *cat* can be processed as three letters and sounds (/kuh/ /a/ /tuh/), or as one letter and one word family (/kuh/ /at/). It takes less cognitive effort to process two units than three. Less effort given to word decoding means more cognitive energy can be applied to reading comprehension.

3. Word families can be thought of as linguistic patterns. They are a combination of written symbols that form a consistent visual and phonological form. Research suggests that the brain is more proficient at recognizing patterns than it is in applying rules (Cunningham, 2004). So using word families taps into the inherent strength of human beings to detect these linguistic patterns in words and transform the patterns into appropriate sounds.

4. Word families are ubiquitous. You will find word families worth teaching and learning in nearly all English words. Edward Fry (1998) found that the 38 most common word families could be found in 654 one-syllable English words. Moreover, those 38 word families are embedded in literally thousands of multisyllabic English words.

Clearly, teaching students phonics through word families gives them a tool for unlocking the sound of a tremendous number of words they will encounter in their reading.

Teaching Word Families

Word families are best taught one family at a time, adding other families as children become successful in identifying the words. That is, we suggest teaching one or, at the most, two word families at a time. Select a word family, discuss the nature of the letters and the sounds represented by the letter pattern, and then brainstorm with students words belonging in that word family. These words can be put in a classroom pocket chart (and perhaps in students' word journals), and you can lead your students in reading the words on the chart several times over the course of a day or two. So, for example, if you were teaching the *-ack* word family, the following list of words might find their way to your word family chart.

back	tack	sack
stack	crack	black
cracker	blackboard	backpack

Once students are able to read the words belonging to a word family, you may add to your chart, and intermingle with the initial word set, the new words belonging to a second word family. So, if your next word family was *-uck*, you might alter your original chart to look like this.

back	luck	tack	sack	buck
stuck	stack	cluck	crack	black
tack	truck	slack	chuck	tuck
cracker	lucky	blackboard	woodchuck	backpack

The purpose of adding the second set of words is that if all the words on a chart belong to the same word family, students soon realize that all they have to do is read the first letter or consonant blend or digraph for each word as the remainders of each word rhyme. Adding the second set of words requires students to look through the entire word in order to pronounce it correctly because the word family or phonogram that comes after the initial letter(s) does not always belong to the same word family. We want students to do this in order to get the entire word into their memory.

Once students have practiced the words in a list format, we quickly move them to reading a passage that contains multiple examples of the linguistic unit they are learning. This has resulted in the development of what has been called decodable texts—passages written for the primary purpose of teaching and practicing a word family or other linguistic unit. The decodable texts we have seen written for children leave something to be desired. For example, students are asked to read passages such as the following:

Mr. Zack had a pack on his back. / Mr. Black had a pack on his back.

These texts have very little in common with real stories. There is no storyline, the passage is not interesting, and there is little meaning being conveyed through the text. This seems to be a disingenuous approach to giving students opportunities to practice word families in authentic, engaging, and interesting texts. We agree in principle with the notion of decodable texts. However, when it comes to word family instruction, we think that such texts already exist in authentic and engaging forms for students. Since word families by their very nature rhyme and are found in many words, why not simply use poetry, song lyrics, and rhymes that we find and that we write to give students practice in reading texts containing targeted word families? Instead of Mr. Zack, we'd much prefer to have our students read our adaptation of "Hickory Dickory Dock."

HICKORY DICKORY DACK

The mouse was in need of a snack. / He peeked through the hole.
He peeked through the crack. / Hickory Dickory Dack.

Text that has rhythm and rhyme built into it is a text that young students will love reading again and again. And when they do, they will be developing a clear and deep recognition of the *-ack* phonics word family. They will also be developing another critical reading competency—fluency!

Fluency

* *

On the road to comprehension, fluency is the second competency that must be acquired by students. Fluency refers to the ability to read the words in text (the surface structure) not only accurately but also effortlessly at an appropriate rate, with good phrasing, and appropriate expression that reflects the meaning of the passage (the deep structure). Fluency has been called the bridge from phonics to comprehension (Pikulski & Chard, 2005), and you can see in the previous sentence how reading with fluency involves both reading the surface words in the text well and in a way that reflects the deeper meaning that we, the authors, intend to express.

Fluency involves two critical features: automaticity and prosody. *Automaticity* is the part of fluency related to word recognition. *Prosody* is the connection to comprehension.

Automaticity

Automaticity refers to the ability to read words in text not only accurately but also with near effortlessness, or automatically (LaBerge & Samuels, 1974). The theory of automaticity proposes that humans have a limited amount of attention or cognitive energy. When our attention is applied to one task, it cannot be easily applied to a second task. Think of when you have tried to do two or three things that required your close attention at the same time. It is very likely that you did a poor job on at least one of those tasks.

The task of reading requires readers to do more than one task simultaneously. First, readers must decode the words they encounter as they read. Second, they must construct meaning from the printed words. If a reader has to use too much cognitive energy to decode the words in a text, even if they are read correctly he or she may not have sufficient cognitive resources available to make meaning or comprehend the passage. As a result, comprehension suffers.

We see these readers quite often in our classrooms. They read slowly and exert much effort as they move from one word to the next in a laborious manner. We need students to move beyond mere accuracy in word decoding to automaticity. An excellent example of automaticity is driving a vehicle. Do you recall when you first learned to drive? If you were like us, you thought about every little aspect of the skills involved (i.e., hands in the 10 and 2 positions, when to flip on the turn signal, vigilant watch of the speedometer, and so on). Now, as experienced drivers, we are rarely conscious of how much pressure we apply to the brake or accelerator pedals, how often we stop for a signal, how far we must turn the wheel to round a corner, and so forth. Our attention can be directed at other things, such as finding our destination.

The best example of automaticity in reading is very likely yourself. When you read, you instantly and automatically recognize most of the words with a minimal amount of cognitive effort. Rarely do you have to stop and sound out a word. The consequence of automaticity in word recognition is that you can direct attention to making meaning from the text. How did you, and all of us, develop automaticity in our reading (or any activity in which we manifest some degree of automaticity)? The answer is practice. Automaticity in reading is developed through lots of reading. When we refer to practice in reading, we refer to two kinds of practice: wide practice and deep practice.

- **Wide practice** refers to the kind of reading most of us do as adult proficient readers. We read a book, an article in a magazine, an item in the newspaper, and when we are finished, we move on to the next piece of text. Our students do wide reading in their core reading programs when they read one story, discuss it with classmates, do an extension activity, and then move on to the next story.

- **Deep reading** practice has also been called *repeated reading* (Samuels, 1979) or rehearsal. It is the kind of practice that you might find in athletics or music in which athletes or musicians practice a certain drill or piece of music repeatedly until they can perform it well and automatically. In reading, this means having a student read one relatively short text several times until he or she can read it well. Once one text is mastered, the student moves on to a new text and practices until achieving mastery of it.

A large body of research has shown that when students read texts repeatedly, they improve in word recognition, fluency, and comprehension of those texts. However, and more important, when students move on to other passages they have not previously read, improvement is also noted on those new passages, and overall reading achievement improves (National Reading Panel, 2000; Rasinski, Reutzel, Chard, & Linan-Thompson, in press). In other words, the facilitative effect (automaticity in word recognition) from practicing one passage repeatedly transfers to new passages—real learning takes place when one passage is practiced.

Automaticity is most commonly measured through reading speed—the number of words a student can read correctly in a grade-level passage in a minute (Rasinski, 2010). Generally, we expect first graders to be able to read first-grade material at about 60 words correct per minute by the end of the school year. With each succeeding grade level in the elementary grades, the expectations for reading rate increase. By the end of fifth grade, we expect students to be reading fifth-grade material at approximately 140 words correct per minute.

Research has found a remarkably strong correlation between reading rate and reading comprehension (Rasinski, 2010). We attribute this correlation to automaticity, not speed. As readers become more accurate and automatic in their word recognition, their reading rate will normally increase. As readers become more automatic in their word recognition, they will also be able to devote less attention to word recognition and more to comprehension—thus comprehension also improves along with automaticity and speed of reading.

We want to make it clear here that automaticity is the key element in fluency, not speed. Using reading speed as a measure of fluency and as a proxy measure for comprehension has led many well-meaning educators to confuse fluency with speed. In these classrooms, teachers work with students on using repeated reading to develop their reading speed, not their automaticity. Reading instruction in these classrooms has become something like a NASCAR race—the students' goal for reading fluency is simply to read faster and faster, much like a racecar driver. Reading speed may increase with these students, but it is unlikely that their fluency, comprehension, or general enjoyment of reading will improve.

Prosody

If fluency is a bridge, then automaticity can be viewed as the link to word recognition. Automaticity frees the reader from using too much of his or her cognitive resources on word recognition. The connection to comprehension can be found in the second part of fluency—prosody.

Prosody is a linguistic term for what we might otherwise call reading orally with appropriate phrasing and expression that reflects and enhances the meaning of the passage. It can be thought of as "reading with feeling." Certainly, when we think of a person who is a fluent speaker or reader, we think of someone who can convey meaning with voice as well as words. When readers read orally, they speak loudly and softly, speed up and slow down, pause appropriately

Phonics & Fluency Practice With Poetry © 2012 by Rasinski, Rupley, & Nichols • Scholastic Teaching Resources

in the text to indicate phrase boundaries, pause for dramatic effect, emphasize certain words, syllables, and sounds within words, and change the nature of their voices when reading quotes and dialogue between characters. A reader does this to reflect and access meaning in a passage.

Research has shown that readers' ability to read with prosody in oral reading is closely related to their ability to read with good comprehension in oral and silent reading (National Reading Panel, 2000; Rasinski, 2010). Moreover, research supports the idea that instruction that focuses students' attention on reading with good expression also leads to improvements in overall reading proficiency. Thus, instruction in fluency needs to be aimed not only at developing automaticity in word recognition but also at expressiveness in oral and silent reading. We mention silent reading here because we know that most readers do hear themselves when they read silently; thus, prosody is not limited solely to oral reading.

Expressive or prosodic reading is developed in a variety of ways. First, we need to find texts that lend themselves to prosodic reading—that's where poetry, song lyrics, and rhymes come in. Such rhythmical texts require a reader to read with expression or prosody. Interestingly, informational texts are generally used in many current commercial fluency programs. We feel that informational passages generally do not have a strong sense of voice. Most informational passages are written in third person with the intent of conveying meaning. Imagine reading a passage titled "Cumulus Clouds" or "Igneous Rock" expressively. Don't get us wrong—we are strong advocates of informational texts but not for the purpose of developing fluency.

For working on prosody in reading, we look for text that has a strong voice and that can easily be read aloud or performed. These texts include narrative (story) passages, monologues, dialogues, scripts to be read as readers theater, song lyrics, and of course, poetry and rhymes. To be read well, these texts require the reader to read with good expression. Poetry, song lyrics, and rhymes are particularly conducive to expressive reading and are abundant for the reading-level needs of students in kindergarten through grade five.

Once you have the appropriate texts, you can develop students' expressive reading through modeling expressive reading, assisted reading, and repeated reading.

- **Modeling expressive meaning** simply means that you need to read texts fluently to your students as they follow along silently. Read with good expression and then talk with your students about how you made meaning with your voice. Return to a portion of the text where you inserted a dramatic pause or changed your voice or varied the pace of your reading, reread this part, and discuss how the change in the expressiveness of your reading helped with students' comprehension. You might also occasionally read "disfluently" to your students—too fast, too slow, word-by-word, without expression or appropriate phrasing. Then talk with your students about how this lack of expression made it more difficult for them to comprehend and enjoy what you read. Lead them into a discussion and demonstration of how the text should have been read to help listeners comprehend it.

- **Assisted reading** involves one reader reading with a partner or a group of other readers, especially when the other reader is a fluent reader. When a developing reader reads while listening at the same time to a more fluent reading of the passage (read by an adult, classmate, or group of classmates), he or she will be able to imitate the expressiveness employed by the other reader(s). Assisted reading can be done through choral reading, singing, paired reading with a partner, echo reading with a partner, alternating lines or paragraphs with a partner, and reading while listening to a prerecorded version of the passage on audiotape or as a podcast. In each of these approaches, the developing reader has a model of support of the other voice(s) to assist with word recognition and prosody.

• **Repeated reading** works well in developing prosody as students read a text several times. The goal of each rereading is not only to improve students' word recognition but also to improve the expressiveness of their reading. Often, on an initial reading, the reader may not be able to read the passage with good expression. However, after two or three rehearsals, the reader can read with excellent prosody and may even perform the passage orally for classmates or another audience. As with automaticity, we have found that the prosody developed through the repeated reading of one passage transfers to other passages read orally and silently, and this in turn improves comprehension.

Poetry, Song Lyrics, and Rhymes Provide the Means for More Fluency Instruction

Fluency has not only been called a bridge from phonics to comprehension, it has also been called the neglected goal of the reading program (Allington, 1983). Allington argued that although fluency is important, over the past several decades it has not been part of the regular reading curriculum. He wondered if the reason many students struggled in reading was because this key element of the reading curriculum had not been given sufficient emphasis.

Allington made his call for more fluency instruction three decades ago. Yet a recent study of classrooms in which reading fluency instruction was mandated by the federal literacy initiative called Reading First found that less than five minutes per day were devoted to fluency development even in these classrooms (Gamse, Bloom, Kemple, et al., 2008). We wonder if one of the reasons that the high hopes placed on Reading First to increase reading achievement in these schools was not fully realized is due to the fact that fluency, this critical aspect of reading and bridge to comprehension, continued to be relatively neglected. Moreover, we think that fluency has continued to be neglected because it has been treated in an artificial manner—as repeated reading of informational text for the purpose of reading it fast.

Phonics and fluency are critical to students' development as readers who understand and enjoy what they read. Neither of these factors can be ignored or neglected. The challenge is to find ways to teach phonics and fluency in ways that are central to their purpose, enjoyable, and efficient in their execution. Because of their inherent rhyme and rhythm, we feel that poetry, song lyrics, and rhymes are ideal texts for teaching phonics and fluency in ways that are engaging and authentic. When students perform poetry orally, sing new song lyrics, and recite rhymes out loud, they have to rehearse—and that's repeated reading. And, when students rehearse, the aim of the rehearsal is expressive reading—and that's prosody as well as automaticity. In the remainder of this book, we will show you how you can use poetry, rhymes, and song lyrics to teach phonics *and* fluency together in ways that are effective— and that you and your students will enjoy!

Chapter 2

Why Use Poetry, Song Lyrics, and Rhymes for Reading Instruction?

As we discussed in Chapter 1, we believe that poetry, song lyrics, and rhymes are natural text choices for teaching phonic skills and developing fluency. These beautiful forms of rhythmical language that include traditional poetry, nursery rhymes, song lyrics, jump rope chants, cheers, and other similar forms of language are meant to be read orally as well as silently and have inspired children to read and sing them for years.

Poetry

* *

At one time in American history, poetry was a cornerstone for reading instruction; in more recent years, it has been replaced by other educational approaches and materials for reading (Elster & Hanauer, 2002). Even though other genres of reading may be more prevalent in modern-day classrooms, poetry is making a resurgence in early reading programs. The predictable, controlled, yet challenging vocabulary associated with poems is a natural fit with many early childhood reading approaches (Anderson, Hiebert, Scott, & Wilkinson, 1985; Holdaway, 1979; Snow, Burns, & Griffin, 1998). Because it provides many opportunities to work on word families and to engage in repeated and prosodic reading with students, poetry provides the natural means to develop phonics and fluency (Rasinski, Rupley & Nichols, 2009).

Poetry is one of the more personal genres of writing, and for centuries poets have given us language that is beautiful and evocative. For example, repeated readings of a poem such as "The Road Not Taken" can help develop older students' fluency, prosody, and expression, and it will also allow them to forge a personal connection with the material as they reflect on their various readings of it and how their understanding can evolve with each reading. Following the student's fluent and expressive reading and assurance from the teacher that he or she did so, the bridge to comprehension can be constructed with a simple question such as, "What do you think of this poem?" This will lead to an active discussion in which students realize that there is no one correct answer to the question but that credible answers must be supported by evidence in the text and their own reasoning.

THE ROAD NOT TAKEN *by Robert Frost*

Two roads diverged in a yellow wood,
And sorry I could not travel both
And be one traveler, long I stood
And looked down one as far as I could
To where it bent in the undergrowth;

And both that morning equally lay
In leaves no step had trodden black.
Oh, I kept the first for another day!
Yet knowing how way leads on to way,
I doubted if I should ever come back.

Then took the other, as just as fair,
And having perhaps the better claim,
Because it was grassy and wanted wear;
Though as for that the passing there
Had worn them really about the same,

I shall be telling this with a sigh
Somewhere ages and ages hence:
Two roads diverged in a wood, and I—
I took the one less traveled by,
And that has made all the difference.

Through the thoughtful selection of words, poets show us how word choice and the arrangement of words can be used to create an emotional effect. Poetry, then, serves as a highly motivational text type for developing a love for reading and for language as well as fluency in oral reading (Duthie & Zimet, 1992; Perfect, 1999). For example, each reading of the section below from "The Highwayman" gives readers an even greater appreciation of Noyes's use of metaphor and imagery that evoke a mood of foreboding and dread.

from "THE HIGHWAYMAN: PART 1" *by Alfred Noyes*

The wind was a torrent of darkness among the gusty trees,
The moon was a ghostly galleon tossed upon cloudy seas,
The road was a ribbon of moonlight over the purple moor,
And the highwayman came riding—
    Riding—riding—
The highway man came riding, up to the old inn-door.

Contributing to the motivational nature of poetry is its personal form which allows readers to experience the world in new ways (Norton, 1999). In the next poem, Stevenson's use of imagery helps the reader visualize the changes of the seasons by identifying flowers with the summer and, perhaps unexpectedly for some students, fires with the fall.

 Phonics & Fluency Practice With Poetry © 2012 by Rasinski, Rupley, & Nichols • Scholastic Teaching Resources

AUTUMN FIRES *by Robert Louis Stevenson*

In the other gardens
And all up the vale,
From the autumn bonfires
See the smoke trail!

Pleasant summer over
And all the summer flowers,

The red fire blazes,
The gray smoke towers.

Sing a song of seasons!
Something bright in all!
Flowers in the summer,
Fires in the fall!

When encountering the language of poetry, readers and listeners should be encouraged to have emotional and physical reactions to the words. Poet Laureate Robert Pinsky says that poetry has the ability "to comfort and enliven human beings" (Pinsky, as cited by Keillor, 2004). Poets carefully select words in order to paint their unique pictures. The images created by this tapestry of words allow readers to respond and interpret in their own ways, which makes poetry perfect for interpretative performance. After practicing the delivery of a poem such as Tennyson's "The Deserted House" for a classroom coffeehouse performance, a student will not only develop fluency but also deepen his or her comprehension (and appreciation) of the work.

THE DESERTED HOUSE *by Alfred Tennyson*

Life and Thought have gone away
Side by side,
Leaving door and windows wide:
Careless tenants they!

All within is dark as night:
In the windows is no light;
And no murmur at the door,
So frequent on its hinge before.

Close the door, the shutters close,
Or thro' the windows we shall see
The nakedness and vacancy
Of the dark deserted house.

Come away: no more of mirth
Is here or merry-making sound.
The house was builded of the earth,
And shall fall again to ground.

Come away: for Life and Thought
Here no longer dwell;
But in a city glorious—
A great and distant city—have bought
A mansion incorruptible.
Would they could have stayed with us!

According to Elster and Hanauer (2002), poetry is intended to focus the reader's attention on the language itself and can be of great value in enhancing students' reading pleasure and ability. When our students experience poetry, song lyrics, and rhymes, we should encourage them to explore sound patterns and offer them many opportunities to respond to rhythm, rhyme, alliteration, assonance, and onomatopoeia. Repeatedly reading poetry selections prompts the reader to reflect on deeper levels of meaning and realize that a poem can be interpreted differently with each reading (Norton, 1999).

Sharing poetry should be a joyous event that is pleasant for the teacher and students alike. Poetry reading should be inspirational and nurture enthusiasm to read more. This can occur naturally as the child begins to hear the rhythm of the poetry and the lilt of the voice of the person sharing the poem. The rhyming poem "The Purple Cow" provides a perfect example of a simple, whimsical poem that should be blissful to share. The rhyme, phrasing, and humor in this poem make it a joy to read aloud.

THE PURPLE COW *by Gelett Burgess*

I never saw a Purple Cow, / I never Hope to See One;
But I can tell you, Anyhow, / I'd rather See than Be One.

Poetry that is selected for sharing should be read beautifully and melodically in order to introduce children to the musical quality of language. This provides the setting for exploring language, thus giving students the right motivation to become interested in new words and to enjoy the feel, rhythm, and sound of the words as they are repeated over and over again. In "Grandpa Dropped His Glasses," for example, the reader and listeners are hooked as they anticipate the next appearance of the word *purple*.

GRANDPA DROPPED HIS GLASSES *by Leroy Jackson*

Grandpa dropped his glasses once
In a pot of dye,
And when he put them on again
He saw a purple sky.
Purple fires were rising up
From a purple hill,
Men were grinding purple cider
At a purple mill.

Purple Adeline was playing
With a purple doll;
Little purple dragon flies
Were crawling up the wall.
And at the supper-table
He got crazy as a loon
From eating purple apple dumplings
With a purple spoon.

When using poetry with young learners to explore language and develop fluency with the printed word, you should begin with shared reading and recitation of familiar rhymes and jingles, such as Mother Goose, and old nursery rhymes and songs. With each shared reading, the vitality of the language is enhanced and enlivened (Strickland & Strickland, 1997). The rhythm and rhyme of a known poem such as "Hey! Diddle, Diddle" encourage the reader and listeners to rock their bodies, clap their hands, and shout and sing them again and again!

HEY! DIDDLE, DIDDLE

Hey! Diddle, Diddle! / The cat and the fiddle,
The cow jumped over the moon; / The little dog laughed
To see such sport, / And the dish ran away with the spoon.

Why Use Poetry, Song Lyrics, and Rhymes for Teaching Phonics?

* *

Quite simply, the reason we advocate poetry, song lyrics, and rhymes for teaching phonics is that this genre of writing contains word families, which are the rhyming portions of words. As we previously discussed, one approach for teaching phonics, the analytical approach, recognizes that many words share certain and relatively common spelling patterns that also have consistent pronunciations. Readers who recognize these letter combinations and associate the pronunciation with them can then apply this decoding knowledge to other words within that word family. Readers who can recognize these word families and transfer this knowledge to other words in a family increase their word recognition ability and, as a result, become more fluent readers and comprehenders.

The idea, then, is to teach young readers these word families so that they can use this knowledge to quickly and effortlessly recognize words that share these spelling patterns while reading. This approach to phonics instruction has been recognized and endorsed by leading scholars in reading (Adams, 1990; Cunningham, 2004; Ehri, 2005; Gaskins, Ehri, Cress, O'Hara, & Donnelly, 1996–1997; Gunning, 1995; Snow, Burns, & Griffin, 1998). The spelling patterns can take a variety of forms—prefixes, suffixes, and Latin and Greek roots, are just a few. However, we believe that the most important patterns to teach early readers are the vowel-consonant combinations called word families, phonograms, or rimes. Again, a word family is simply the part of a syllable that begins with the vowel and contains any subsequent letters. When a word family is placed in one-syllable words (or at the end of multisyllabic words), it creates rhyming words. As you can see, even a short and simple rhyme such as "Georgy Porgy" contains several word families.

GEORGY PORGY

Georgy Porgy, pudding and pie, / Kissed the girls and made them *cry*;
When the boys came *out* to *play*, / Georgy Porgy *ran away*.

Word Families: *-ay, -y , -an, -out*

These letter combinations are the part of a syllable that begins with the vowel and contains any letters that follow it; for example, the *-at* in *hat* and *cat* is a word family, as is the *-ight* in *flight* and *sight*. As we mentioned in Chapter 1, there are hundreds of word families worth teaching, and students who can recognize these word families in single and multisyllabic words have the ability to process such words rapidly, accurately, and efficiently. The beloved nursery rhyme "Jack and Jill" contains a treasure trove of repeated word families.

JACK AND JILL

Jack and *Jill went* up the *hill*, / To fetch a *pail* of water;
Jack fell down and broke his *crown*, / And *Jill* came tumbling after.

Then up *Jack got* and home did *trot,* / As fast as he could caper.

He *went* to *bed* to *mend* his head / With vinegar and *brown* paper.

Word Families: *-ack, -ell, -ent, -end, -ill, -ail, -ing, -ed, -ot, -own*

While word families are commonly taught through word lists and decodable texts by teachers around the country, we again emphasize that the best types of text to support word family instruction are poetry, song lyrics, and rhymes. Rhythmic language in these texts draw attention to targeted word families that are authentic and engaging for children. As a final example, the following rhyme would be ideal for teaching, practicing, and enjoying the *-ot, -old,* and *-ay,* word families.

PEAS PORRIDGE HOT

Peas porridge *hot* / Peas porridge *cold*

Peas porridge in the *pot* / Nine *days old.*

Some like it *hot,* / Some like it *cold,*

Some like it in the *pot,* / Nine days *old.*

Why Use Poetry, Song Lyrics, and Rhymes for Teaching Fluency?

* *

Repeated oral reading of texts (rehearsal), combined with modeling fluent reading and supporting students while reading orally by reading with them, have been identified as key methods for teaching reading fluency (Kuhn & Stahl, 2000; National Reading Panel, 2000; Rasinski, 2010; Rasinski & Hoffman, 2003). Studies have found that repeated reading leads to improvements in student automaticity, word recognition accuracy, reading rate, expressive and meaningful reading, reading comprehension, and confidence in reading. Such reading capabilities apply not only to the passages students have practiced, but they also transfer to new, never-before-seen texts.

Although the value of repeated readings has been well established, the mode of implementing it remains an issue. Many reading programs that promote fluency development primarily engage students in rote and somewhat mindless oral repetitions of texts for the primary purpose of increasing reading speed. Elster and Hanauer, however, note that reading poetry is different from story reading and other text types and that teachers naturally encourage multiple readings of poetry for expression or prosody. Poetry reading emphasizes the performance and the more aesthetic experiences with reading (2002). After assigning "There Was a Crooked Man" as a performance piece for your students, imagine how repeated readings of the rhyme will not only improve their fluency but also spark their imaginations as they work to bring the poem to life for themselves or an audience.

THERE WAS A CROOKED MAN

There was a crooked man,
And he went a crooked mile,
He found a crooked sixpence,
Against a crooked stile;

He bought a crooked cat,
Which caught a crooked mouse,
And they all lived together
In a little crooked house.

The prosodic, performance, and aesthetic features of poetry, song lyrics, and rhymes are the primary reasons we have identified them as natural text types for improving fluency. If performing orally is a goal of repeated reading, then poetry, song lyrics, and rhymes are the appropriate texts because they can be performed for an audience. As Elster and Hanaeur note, rhythmic text promotes learner involvement through expressive reading and immediate rereading and by encouraging children to read along or to act out the text. After hearing an expressive reading and rereading of a rhyme such as "Whisky Frisky," younger children will literally jump at the chance to act out the squirrel's adventures. As the italicized words in the text show, the rhyme contains the following word families: *-am, -ack, -ail, -ap, -ell, -op, -ow.*

WHISKY FRISKY

Whisky Frisky / Hippity-*Hop*
Up he goes / To the *treetop*!
Whirly, Twirly, / Round and round,
Down he *scampers* / To the ground.

Furly, Curly, / What a *tail*!
Tall as a feather, / Broad as a *sail*!
Where's his supper? / In the *shell*,
Snap, cracky, / Out it *fell*.

Poetry, song lyrics, and rhymes can easily be performed, even if the performer is someone reading a poem to himself or herself. Many poets write their poems to be performed orally for an audience. That is why we have poetry slams, poetry cafes, poetry readings, and poetry parties. Unfortunately, reading curricula are dominated by informational and narrative texts—poetry, song lyrics, and rhymes have been given a secondary or, in some cases, even a tertiary position. We feel that students are missing out on reading activities that allow them to appreciate the beauty of language from a number of vantage points, including meaning, sound, rhythm, and expression. A short text such as the familiar rhyme below contains an abundance of teaching opportunities to promote fluency and phonics, including work with the word families *-ell* and *-ow.*

MISTRESS MARY, QUITE CONTRARY

Mistress Mary, quite contrary, how does your garden grow?
With cockle shells, and silver bells, and pretty maids all in a row.

Exposing children to the beauty, humor, and vitality of poetic language cannot begin too early and should come about naturally. The words used in poetry, songs, and nursery rhymes are a breath of freshness for language and make reading them and listening to them a pure delight.

The Appeal of Poetry, Song Lyrics, and Rhymes

* *

The rhythmic nature of poetry, song lyrics, and rhymes gives this text genre a musical quality that for centuries has had a universal appeal to children and that provides levels of support and scaffolding for the child just learning to read. The motivational attributes of this text type support the learning of rich vocabulary and complex ideas and encourages readers to be persistent. Poems such as "A Home on the Range" and "Twinkle, Twinkle, Little Star" beg to be sung, and the lyrical nature of these poems provides a rich rhythm that is appealing to young readers and their predictable patterns scaffold reading.

A HOME ON THE RANGE

(traditional cowboy song)

Oh, give me a home where the buffalo roam,
Where the deer and the antelope play;
Where seldom is heard a discouraging word
And the skies are not cloudy all day.

CHORUS: *Home, home on the range,*
Where the deer and the antelope play;
Where seldom is heard a discouraging word
And the skies are not cloudy all day.

Where the air is so pure, the zephyrs
    so free,
The breezes so balmy and light,
That I would not exchange my home on
    the range
For all the cities so bright.

[*CHORUS*]

The red man was pressed from this part
    of the West,
He's likely no more to return
To the banks of Red River where seldom
    if ever
Their flickering campfires burn.

[*CHORUS*]

How often at night when the heavens are bright
With the light from the glittering stars,
Have I stood here amazed and asked as I gazed
If their glory exceeds that of ours.

[*CHORUS*]

Oh, I love these wild flowers in this dear land
    of ours;
The curlew I love to hear scream;
And I love the white rocks and the antelope flocks
That graze on the mountaintops green.

[*CHORUS*]

Oh, give me a land where the bright
    diamond sand
Flows leisurely down the stream;
Where the graceful white swan goes
    gliding along
Like a maid in a heavenly dream.

[*CHORUS*]

Then I would not exchange my home on
    the range,
Where the deer and the antelope play;
Where seldom is heard a discouraging word
And the skies are not cloudy all day.

 Phonics & Fluency Practice With Poetry © 2012 by Rasinski, Rupley, & Nichols • Scholastic Teaching Resources

TWINKLE, TWINKLE, LITTLE STAR *by Jane Taylor*

Twinkle, twinkle, little star,
How I wonder what you are!
Up above the world so high,
Like a diamond in the sky.

When the glorious sun is set,
When the grass with dew is wet,
Then you show your little light,
Twinkle, twinkle, all the night.

Then the traveler in the dark,
Thanks you for your tiny spark!
He could not see which way to go,
If you did not twinkle so.

In the dark blue sky you keep,
And often through my curtains peep,
For you never shut your eye,
Till the sun is in the sky.

As your bright and tiny spark,
Lights the traveler in the dark,
Though I know not what you are,
Twinkle, twinkle, little star.

Poetry, song lyrics, and rhymes are meant to be heard even when the reader is the only audience. Robert Pinsky captures the essence of the physical nature of rhythmic language (cited by Keillor, 2004):

> *The medium of poetry is not words, the medium of poetry is not lines—it is the motion of air inside the human body, coming out through the chest and the voice box and through the mouth to shape sounds that have meaning. It's bodily.*

The more we can make learning a multisensory experience, the more likely that struggling learners will meet success. The physical nature of poetry, song lyrics, and rhymes taps directly into a multisensory approach to learning. As Emily Dickinson stated, "If I read a book and it makes my whole body so cold no fire can ever warm me, I know *that* is poetry."

Poetry, song lyrics, and rhymes not only give us insights into language, but they also provide opportunities to deepen our understanding of our culture. Cultural literacy is an important goal of schooling: So many poems reflect who we are as a society and what some of our greatest aspirations are. Reading the poetry of Walt Whitman, Emily Dickinson, Carl Sandburg, Langston Hughes, Maya Angelou, and so many other poets allows students to examine the meaning of the American experience from differing points of view.

Poems, songs, and nursery rhymes also serve as the beloved right of childhood. Children can immerse themselves in a world populated by fairies, elves, and talking animals in which the rhythmic language provides a form of expression that fuels their imagination. Writers of poetry, songs, and rhymes appear to magically arrange words in a manner that paints a picture of sounds and language that helps the reader hear, see, and feel the experience in a unique way. For example, Walter De La Mare's repetition of words and phrases ("sure-sure-sure," "Tap-tapping," and "at all, at all, at all") sets a tone of urgency and makes the words tumble from a reader's mouth. It's an imaginative poem that a reader wants to read over and over.

SOME ONE *by Walter De La Mare*

Someone came knocking
At my wee, small door;
Someone came knocking;
I'm sure-sure-sure;
I listened, I opened,
I looked to left and right,
But nought there was a-stirring
In the still dark night;

Only the busy beetle
Tap-tapping in the wall,
Only from the forest
The screech-owl's call,
Only the cricket whistling
While the dewdrops fall,
So I know not who came knocking,
At all, at all, at all.

Many poems give children fresh insights into the world. Poetry encourages them to play with words and to realize how words can create images and why word choice is so important. Through poetry, children discover the power and beauty of words (Strickland & Strickland, 1997). Children given the gift of poetry improve their ability to enjoy, appreciate, and interpret life (Godden, 1988). Teachers and parents who read poetry and nursery rhymes to their children are contributing to a foundation for lifetime reading and nurturing a taste for poetry.

It is critically important that teachers and students understand the motivational influence that poetry, song lyrics, and rhymes have on writing and reading. Teachers can enhance their students' love of poetry, songs, and rhymes by modeling and manifesting their own appreciation of them (Graves, 1992; Parr & Campbell, 2006; Wilson, 1994). Learners who do not engage in the joys of such texts miss out on the opportunity to discover how rewarding and enjoyable they can be in all aspects of literacy. The true motivation for learning and using poetry, song lyrics, and rhymes is the realization that they have an abundance of positive benefits. They can give students immediate success and confidence in literacy activities, encourage language and word play, connect reading and writing, and demonstrate the importance and creativity of word choice and word order (Parr & Campbell, 2006; Routman, 2001). And, as the lessons and activities in this book show, poetry, song lyrics, and rhymes are a wonderful text choice for making phonics and fluency instruction authentic, engaging, and effective.

Chapter 3

The Big Picture: Implementing a Poetry Curriculum for Phonics and Fluency

Phonics (word recognition) and reading fluency are absolutely essential in developing readers who are fluent and proficient in comprehension. When students reach a level of fluency in word recognition and have an understanding of the prosodic features of language, they become free from the constraints of decoding and are able to enjoy the pleasures of reading and the opportunity to think creatively and critically about what they read. Rhyming poetry is an ideal vehicle for helping students develop mastery in all three critical competencies (word recognition, fluency, and comprehension) and have fun while doing so. The use of rhyming poetry also expands opportunities for students to appreciate language and learn about the world, while at the same exploring the wonderful uses of words.

The question at this point, then, is "How can I teach rhyming poetry, song lyrics, and rhymes as an integral part of my curriculum for developing phonics, fluency, and other essential components of my reading curriculum?" In many classrooms today, rhyming poetry is used as a tangential add-on to fill time or as a brief respite from or transition between other "more important" parts of the curriculum. To use poetry as an integral part of your reading curriculum, you need to provide scaffolded instruction that allows students to learn to read assigned poems fluently and, at the same time, develop mastery of individual words within each poem under your guidance or that of their peers.

In this chapter, we present four different approaches for building phonics skills, reading fluency, and comprehension during the reading and enjoyment of poetry, songs, and rhymes.

1. Daily Poem
2. Three-Day Phonics and Poetry Routine
3. Five-Day Fluency Poetry Party Routine
4. Fluency Development Lesson

As you can see, these lessons range from one day to one week. Yet, regardless of its length, each lesson shares the following common core elements:

- enjoyment of poetry and songs for their own sake
- focus on the meaning of the poems and songs
- focus on making meaning through oral performance and student participation with positive encouragement
- concentration on the words within poems and songs—both word family words and interesting literary words that poets use in their writing
- teacher modeling of fluent reading
- rehearsal or repeated reading of poetry by students
- assisted reading by reading with others
- community building through group reading of poetry and performing for others

Daily Poem

* *

Many primary grade teachers open the school day with a daily poem. The teacher and students may read a thematic, funny, or inspirational poem chorally once, twice, or three times as the day begins. Then the poem is put on visual display for children to read on their own or again in unison when lining up for lunch, coming in from recess, or just before leaving for the day. This is not only a wonderful way to start each day but is also a great activity to continue throughout the day, with frequent repetition and less formal instruction. For instance, you might try the following schedule for reading a daily poem.

Selection of a poem to which children can relate and which has relevance.

- Choose a poem for each day of the school year. For example, on the day after your class has been invaded by a bee, fly, or other annoying insect, have your students learn to read and enjoy "There Was an Old Man With a Beard" by Edward Lear. Put the poem on a chart or another form of visual display. We like to use an easel with pages that we flip daily because we can return to a previously read poem or song and compare and contrast it with a new poem or song we have just introduced.

THERE WAS AN OLD MAN WITH A BEARD *by Edward Lear*

There was an Old Man with a beard, / Who said, "It is just as I feared!—
Two Owls and a Hen, four Larks and a Wren,
Have all built their nests in my beard!"

Read the poem to model its prosodic features and pronunciation of the words.

- Chorally read the poem with your class two or three times at the beginning of the day. Point out words that rhyme and other interesting words and put these words on display in a separate chart (or word wall). List the words vertically so students can note the similarities in the spelling of rhyming words.

Read the poem frequently over the course of the day to facilitate word memory and prosody features. Read the word list to "keep the words in front of students" and to promote recognition.

- Read the poem and word list twice more before morning recess (e.g., boys read once, girls read once).

- Read the poem and word list again after returning from recess (e.g., alternate the reading of lines between boys and girls—or use some other form of grouping).

- In a cheerful voice, read the poem and word list together before lunch.

- Read the poem as a group after lunch, but this time, use softer voices to get ready for the afternoon.

Use repeated reading combined with movement to enhance memorization of the poem and revisit it as needed for review and to relate the topic, words, and gestures to other poems that will be used later.

- Invite individuals and groups of two and three students to read the poem at the end of the day in an impromptu poetry slam. Encourage children to develop hand and body movements to go along with their performances.

- Retire the poem to the back of the room, perhaps to a poetry corner, where students can continue to read it on subsequent days.

- Every Friday (or as often as your schedule allows) bring back the retired poems so that students can read and perform their favorites again and again.

You will notice that we have simply expanded the notion of the daily poem by giving students the opportunity to read it repeatedly throughout the school day in different ways and with different voices. By focusing on the words in the daily poem we have also given children the opportunity to examine the words for patterns and interest. The repeated readings of the poem develop fluency for students and the harvesting and reading of words from the poem will strengthen their word recognition skills.

This format is very flexible, and you will probably see many other opportunities—to add additional readings; do other word activities, such as sorting the words by certain sounds, letters, or letter patterns; and engage in other instructional activities around the poem. You might also send the poem and its word list home for further reading and enjoyment by children and their families. The key idea is that we need to give students the opportunity to enjoy language and to master certain short texts. That sense of accomplishment that comes from being able to read a text well cannot be underestimated, especially for children who are struggling to become proficient readers.

Three-Day Phonics and Poetry Routine

* *

The Three-Day Phonics and Poetry Routine is one approach for making poetry a more integral part of your phonics program. In this routine, you will intentionally engage your students in instructional conversations about word families and prosodic reading while they are learning the poem at the same time. Here's how the 10–15 minute routine works on each of the three days.

Day 1

On the first day, identify a target word family, demonstrate its spelling and sound, and then together with students brainstorm words that belong to that word family. Record the words and then place them on the Word Family Word Wall. Several times over the course of the day, read this list of words with students, talk about the words, and add other words that belong to that family. Here's how the lesson might go.

TEACHER: Today, we're going to study the *-ay* word family. (*Writes* -ay *on the board so every student can see the spelling and then pronounces it again.*) What words can you think of that are part of the *-ay* word family?

LIAM: *Day, say,* and *may.*

TEACHER: Those are excellent choices. (*Records each word to add to the word wall.*) Hannah, which words can you think of that are part of the *-ay* word family?

HANNAH: How about *pay, play,* and *stay*? And *pray*, too.

TEACHER: Very good. I'll add those words to our Word Family Word Wall. (*Records each word to add to the word wall.*) Now, who can think of multisyllabic words— words with more than one syllable—for the *-ay* word family?

MAX: *Daylight. Playmate. Monday.*

TEACHER: Thanks, Max. I'll add those words to the word wall, too.

Day 2

The second day moves word family instruction from words in isolation to words in the context of rhyming poetry. Display a few rhymes that contain the word family for students to read.

Creating Original Poems

These rhymes may be original or found poems. Simple rhyming poems are easy and fun to write. The poem "Bikes" shown in the modeling example on the next page was written by a teacher who wanted an additional text for working on the *-ay* word family. Tim wrote "Chester" when he was working with students on the *-est* word family.

CHESTER

My best friend Chester is a real pest. / He pesters his sister and his sister's guest.
He thinks he's a jester, never gives them any rest. / Oh, my friend Chester is a real pest.

This brief text contains nine instances of the *-est* word family—and four are multisyllabic words. The students loved reading that rhyme throughout the day and requested their own copy to take home and share with their families.

Read the rhymes with your students. As you do so, point to each word as it is read, drawing children's visual attention to the words themselves.

Several times throughout the day, read the rhymes with your students, and encourage them to read the rhymes on their own as well. When students have essentially memorized a rhyme, point out individual words in it—including-*ay* words as well as other interesting words such as *little, great,* and *again.*

TEACHER: Yesterday, we talked about the *-ay* word family and thought of some words in that word family. Let's read and find those words on the Word Family Word Wall and read them together. (*Students locate and recite words.*) Great! Now, let's look at these rhymes on the board and read them together. (*Points to each -ay word in the rhyme as it is read.*) Each of these rhymes contain several *-ay* words.

RAIN, RAIN, GO AWAY

Rain, rain, go away, / Come again another day, / Little Johnny wants to play.

BIKES

Bikes are to ride / All of the day / Places to go / So far away
Sidewalks and paths / Places to stray / Bikes are to ride / What a great way to play!

TEACHER: Which words in the *-ay* word family do you see in these rhymes?

ALEXIS: "Rain, Rain, Go Away" has *away, day,* and *play.*

TEACHER: (*Underlines those words in the rhyme.*) That's right. All those words belong to the *-ay* word family. Who can tell me some of the *-ay* words in the poem, "Bikes"? (*Underlines words as students volunteer them: day, away, stray, way, play.*)

Word Whoppers

Word Whoppers are a great way for isolating words within a display text. A word whopper can be made by simply taking a half sheet of card stock (5.5-inches by 8.5-inches) and cutting a horizontal window in the center. Then attach a card stock handle to the sheet so that it can be held up to the chart. With a Word Whopper, a teacher or students can isolate words from a text to focus attention on the word and also to challenge students to read the word with the surrounding context hidden.

 # Day 3

Have your students read and reread the poem or poems you've introduced in a variety of ways. For example, begin with an echo read of a poem where you read it line by line. Students echo your reading of each line while focusing on the written text. Next, do a whole-group choral reading of the poem. Then break students into groups and have each group read different parts of the poem. Pairs and trios might also read the poem to each other. Students might also want to record their readings on a recording computer or recorder. Solo silent or oral reading of the poem is another option. Next, guide students in selecting interesting words from the poem. This of course will include many of the word family words, but, again, it also may include other words; for example, with the poems "Rain, Rain, Go Away" and "Bikes," the list might include other words such as *again, little, great, places, far,* and *paths.* Write these words on chart paper to display in the classroom and read and reread the words. The repeated readings and work will develop students' accuracy and automaticity in word recognition.

Follow-Up Activities

Once you've read and recited the poem repeatedly, use various follow-up activities, such as word sorting (Bear, Invernizzi, Templeton, & Johnston, 2007) and word ladders to draw students' attention to the words and the structural features within them.

- **Word Sorting:** Students can sort the words according to a variety of categories, including words that do and do not rhyme, words that have one or more than one syllable, words that contain the *s* sound and words that don't, words that represent things and words that do not, words that contain a word within them and words that do not, and so on. Each time students sort the words, they are practicing the words again, but with each sort, they are examining the words from a different perspective that requires a deeper analysis of the words and that leads them to develop a mastery of the words.

- **Word Ladders:** In a word ladder, students start with one word and then create a series of new words by adding, dropping, or changing one letter according to your directions. While making new words, talk with students about the meaning of the new words as well as how changing one letter resulted in the creation of the new word. Here's an example of a word ladder that incorporates the *-ay* word family:

say > lay > play > pay > pat > pad > had > hat > hay

Subsequent Days

The three-day routine continues with other word families and poems containing the word families. As the word wall expands, you might group words belonging to one word family together. You may also want to have another chart or word wall in which the word families are mixed up to some degree. This will challenge students to visually analyze the words more fully. As we discussed earlier, if words belonging to one word family are grouped together, students will not have to analyze those words deeply because they will recognize that all the words in the group have the same letter pattern and sound. When the words are mixed up, students have to fully examine each word in order to sound it out.

Once the words are displayed on the word wall, you may want to have students work on their own to sort them into word family groups. Again, this will require them to examine the full set of words for common patterns.

Five-Day Fluency Poetry Party Routine

* *

Clearly, you can see how rhyming poetry and songs can be used to enhance and supplement phonics instruction. Rhyming poetry can also be employed for improving students' reading fluency (both automaticity and prosody). The Five-Day Fluency Poetry Party Routine is one way to do this. Since the emphasis in this routine is on fluency rather than on phonics or word families, it is not critical that the poems align with any particular word family. Rather, you should look for poems at an appropriate level of challenge and interest for your students. You can use some of the poems in Chapter 2, or use them as inspiration to come up with ideas for other poems.

In this routine, students will eventually be performing their assigned poems for an audience. The last day of each week in this routine is devoted to a poetry party in which students will celebrate their hard work of learning the poems earlier in the week. Thus, it is important that you talk with them in advance about the appropriate protocol (procedures and behavior) for a "poetry party." Demonstrate and practice with students the appropriate protocol for performing and listening. Performers do the following:

- Stand or sit straight and tall, no slouching.

- Read your poem but don't hold it in front of your face.

- Perform with a voice loud enough for all to hear.

- Be sure to read with expression.

Audience members do the following:

- Listen attentively and politely. No side talk.

- Greet each performance with polite applause or other form of recognition (e.g., clicking of fingers).

- Make a positive comment about the performance when prompted by the teacher after it ends.

We highly recommend you model these responses and practice them with students so they become a procedure and then a routine for reading and listening to poetry.

You can organize the poetry you want your students to learn and to perform in any way. For instance, you might celebrate a different poet each week of the year. Imagine if one week your class celebrated the work of Robert Louis Stevenson. The poems shown below could be included in the corpus of poetry from which individuals or groups of students could choose. If students are performing as a group, they will have to negotiate which parts will be read by individuals and which parts might be read by more than one reader.

TO ANY READER

As from the house your mother sees / You playing round the garden trees,
So you may see, if you will look / Through the windows of this book,

Another child, far, far away, / And in another garden, play.
But do not think you can at all, / By knocking on the window, call

That child to hear you. He intent / Is all on his play-business bent.
He does not hear; he will not look, / Nor yet be lured out of this book.

For, long ago, the truth to say, / He has grown up and gone away,
And it is but a child of air / That lingers in the garden there.

THE WIND

I saw you toss the kites on high / And blow the birds about the sky;
And all around I heard you pass, / Like ladies' skirts across the grass—
O wind, a-blowing all day long, / O wind, that sings so loud a song!

I saw the different things you did, / But always you yourself you hid.
I felt you push, I heard you call, / I could not see yourself at all—
O wind, a-blowing all day long, / O wind, that sings so loud a song!

O you that are so strong and cold, / O blower, are you young or old?
Are you a beast of field and tree, / Or just a stronger child than me?
O wind, a-blowing all day long, / O wind, that sings so loud a song!

MY SHADOW

I have a little shadow that goes in and out with me,
And what can be the use of him is more than I can see.
He is very, very like me from the heels up to the head;
And I see him jump before me, when I jump into my bed.

The funniest thing about him is the way he likes to grow—
Not at all like proper children, which is always very slow;
For he sometimes shoots up taller like an india-rubber ball,
And he sometimes goes so little that there's none of him at all.

He hasn't got a notion of how children ought to play,
And can only make a fool of me in every sort of way.
He stays so close behind me, he's a coward you can see;
I'd think shame to stick to nursie as that shadow sticks to me!

One morning, very early, before the sun was up,
I rose and found the shining dew on every buttercup;
But my lazy little shadow, like an errant sleepy-head,
Had stayed at home behind me and was fast asleep in bed.

On following weeks, other classic poets can be celebrated as well as more contemporary poets, such as Shel Silverstein, Jack Prelutsky, David Harrison, Rob Pottle, and Brod Baggert. Other ways to organize your poetry include seasons of the year, holidays, or topic (e.g., courage, weather, funny poems, and so on).

Here's the daily lesson plan for this routine:

Days 1–2: Introduction (*10–20 minutes*)

Allow students to choose a poem they would like to learn during the week from a limited set that you have developed based on your students' reading capabilities. Give them the opportunity to work on a poem individually or with a partner.

You can either make a copy of each poem for every student and for yourself, or you can display the poem for your class to see it as you read it. Document cameras and LCD projectors are a great use of new technology that allows students to view texts without your having to resort to transparencies or a Power Point presentation.

Read each poem in an expressive voice and ask students to follow along silently. Then read the poem together chorally with the class. Next, talk about the meaning of the poem and any interesting words it contains. Students can highlight these words for later recognition and discussion about why they found these words interesting or meaningful. This focuses students' attention on comprehension and vocabulary before moving into the practice phase of the lesson. Repeat the process for each poem chosen by your students. Ask students to take their individual poem home and practice reading it with their family. Remind students that they will be performing their assigned poems in a few days. Tell them to begin thinking about how they might perform it.

Days 3–4: Rehearsal (*10 minutes each day*)

Individually or with a partner, students practice their poem and listen to classmates read their poems. The focus should be on reading the assigned poem expressively in order to convey meaning and enjoyment to an audience.

Start each rehearsal period with a very brief mini-lesson. Remind students, and demonstrate for them, that the focus is expression and meaning, not reading speed. At the end of each rehearsal, you might ask selected students to give a brief status report on their reading and perhaps to read their poem to the class. Provide positive feedback on the students' reading by pointing out specific features they performed well. Saying "Good job!" is too vague; say, "Chris, when you read the lines about how the old man felt, I could see him in my mind and feel as he felt about his dog." Such specificity helps students determine exactly what they did well and what can be used for future applications and reinforcement: "Chris, read that part the way you did when you read about the man and his dog."

During these brief rehearsal periods, you should be monitoring students' practice. Roam the room, listen to them practice, provide feedback. You may want to engage in paired reading with students who are experiencing some difficulty in learning the poem. By adding your voice to theirs, you will be providing them with additional support and modeling that will help them succeed in learning to read the poem.

❖ Day 5: The Grand Performance *(20–30 minutes)*

The last day of the week is usually a perfect time for a grand performance of poetry, and the grand performance is usually a great way to end the week. Set the stage by decorating your room as best you can to give it a coffeehouse atmosphere. Bring in a bar stool for performers to sit on if they like. Set up a microphone (real or facsimile) at the front of the room. You might also want to have a music stand for students to place their poem on when they perform. Also encourage students to bring in various accoutrements to add to the atmosphere. They might bring in bongos and tambourines and dress in various ways (e.g., all black) to make the day and the performance a special one. Invite parents, the principal, other classes and teachers, and other guests to attend. Encourage guests to share a favorite poem of their own if they would like. If it's feasible, ask parents to bring treats to enjoy. Since this is a coffeehouse, hot chocolate or another drink is very appropriate. Also light, quiet snacks can also contribute to making the poetry party a special event.

Remind students of the ground rules for good performances and appropriate audience behavior. Then invite students (and guests) to perform their poem. You (or a student) may act as the emcee and try to make the coffeehouse a special and authentic event. Begin with an introduction to the week's poems. Prepare an agenda for the poetry party in advance so students know the order in which they will perform. And perform a poem yourself—perhaps one tied to the season or time of year.

If you have a document camera and projector available, bring it out and let performers project an enlarged copy of their poem for the audience to read silently as they perform it. This makes each poetry performance an opportunity for assisted reading.

To add variety, punctuate students' performances with other activities. Add a familiar song or two to the party. Perform a choral reading of a favorite poem from a previous week. It can be a wonderful treat to play a recording of a poem by a special guest who is not present. Be sure that when these other poems and songs are shared, the written text is displayed for students and the audience to read along on their own. After the poetry performances are over, students can enjoy their snacks and bask in the knowledge that, for a few moments each week, they are the stars of their classroom.

Beyond the First Week

* * * * * * * * * * * * * * * * * * * *

The Poetry Party should be a weekly, or at the very least, a biweekly event. Variations can include the group writing and reading of poems or singing songs. We have found that a group of four students is ideal for this variation. The students in the group can either read or sing together, or each member can take a part to read or sing. The primary focus is always on the authentic use of poetry for performing and enjoying in the same way that adults enjoy poetry at a coffeehouse or poetry slam. But underlying the authentic performance is fundamentally sound instruction (Rasinski, 2010): You are modeling fluent reading for students; students are engaging in repeated reading with the focus not on reading speed but on communicating meaning (comprehension); students are engaging in assisted reading as they share their text with you and others; they are also doing assisted reading when they follow along and read silently while the poems are being performed by others. Using this lesson format, or some variation of it, on a regular and sustained basis will develop fluent readers who also have a love of language through poetry.

Fluency Development Lesson *(15–20 minutes daily)*

* *

For most normally achieving students, the Five-Day Fluency Poetry Party Routine is an excellent way to develop and maintain fluency. Some students who struggle in reading need more intensive (Tier 2) fluency instruction. For these students, we recommend the Fluency Development Lesson or FDL (Rasinski, Padak, Linek & Sturtevant, 1994). The FDL is a 15–20 minute daily lesson in which students work intensively on one poem or song per day, practicing it until they can read it fluently and with feeling. The lesson format follows a regular routine that starts with you, the teacher, taking responsibility for reading the daily poem and gradually shifting responsibility for the reading to students. The lesson can be broken down into the following steps.

1. Introduce a new short text (or two) and read it to students two or three times while they follow along silently. Short, predictable poems and songs are ideal for the lesson.

2. With students, discuss the nature and content of the passage as well as the quality of your reading of the passage.

3. Read the passage chorally several times with students. Antiphonal reading (i.e., breaking the text into parts that are read by different groups in the classroom—for example, boys do certain parts, girls do other parts, and still other parts are read by both boys and girls together) and other variations are used to create variety and maintain engagement. Such variations include your reading a line, a student or students reading the next line, and continuing this way until the end of the text; you read a line inappropriately (too slowly, poor phrasing, too fast, and so on) and students read the line so it communicates meaning; and you read a portion of a line and students finish reading it.

4. Organize students into pairs or trios. Each student practices the passage three times while his or her partner listens and provides support and encouragement.

5. Individuals and groups of students perform their reading for the class or another audience, such as another class, a parent visitor, the school principal, or another teacher.

6. You and your students then choose 4 to 6 interesting words from the text to add to the individual students' word banks and/or the classroom word wall. Words are written for the word bank and can be assembled with clip rings for individual students.

7. Students engage in 5–10 minutes of word-study activities (e.g., word sorts with word bank words, word ladders, flashcard practice, defining words, word games, and so on). As with all activities, you demonstrate and request student responses so they clearly understand the procedures.

8. Students take a copy of the passage home to practice with parents and other family members. To assure that they practice at home, place a symbol or box at the bottom of the copy and have parents check that the student practiced the passage. "Smiley faces" work well for younger children and parents can circle or check it.

9. The following day, students read the passage from the previous day to you or a partner for accuracy and fluency. Words from the previous day are also read, reread, grouped, and sorted by students and/or groups of students.

10. The instructional routine then begins again with step #1 and a new poem or song.

The FDL is the core reading-fluency instructional strategy employed at the Kent State University Reading Clinic for struggling readers. We have seen students make remarkable progress in their reading fluency and overall reading proficiency by using this lesson on a daily basis in as little as five weeks.

The lessons we have shared with you are simply models of poetry lessons that you can use or adapt to your own instructional needs and style of teaching. There is no one correct way to teach poetry. Indeed, we invite you to create your own poetry lessons that match the specific instructional needs of your students. Here's a sample lesson that teacher Tara Johnson developed that focuses on word families.

Sample Lesson

Lesson Rationale

The learner will develop and apply enabling strategies and skills to read and write. Self-monitor decoding by using one or two decoding strategies (e.g., beginning letters, rimes, length of word, ending letters).

Research Citation

"When describing how children decode short words, we emphasized the importance of patterns. The patterns in short words are onsets and rimes. When good readers encounter an unfamiliar short word in their reading, they look at the beginning letters—the onset—and assign it a pronunciation. Next, they look at the rime—the vowel and what follows—and assign it a pronunciation. They blend these two parts together to produce a reasonable pronunciation for the word." (Cunningham, 2009, p. 126)

Learning Objectives

The students will be able to identify patterns of onsets and rimes. The students will use onsets and rimes to construct and decode words to use in writing and reading their own rhymes.

Objective Stated for Students

"Has anyone ever noticed a special pattern with some words having the same ending sound and letters but a different beginning sound? And, if you have noticed that, then you may have also noticed some words have the same beginning sounds and letter(s) but different ending sounds. Can someone tell me which of these sound and letter patterns you would find in a rhyme? Today, we are going to learn more about these sounds and letter patterns and how we can use these patterns to make new words. So, at the end of this lesson, each of you will be able to write your very own rhyme and share it with the class."

Lesson Opening

To open the lesson, I will have the students join me in the reading circle, and we will talk about rhymes. Some probing/cueing questions I will ask them to consider are: *What makes a rhyme? Where can we find rhymes (e.g., books, music, other printed sources)? Is a rhyme different from a poem? Are rhymes short or long? Does anyone have a favorite rhyme to share?*

As a whole-class group, we will be reading "Rock-a-Bye Baby." I will have all the students verbalize the word families of focus from this nursery rhyme.

Lesson Body

Teacher Input: After reading the nursery rhyme, I will model the learning objective by first showing the students a spelling pattern of one word family/rime, saying the rime, and then having students repeat the rime. For example, I might create a chart showing the *-ock* word family.

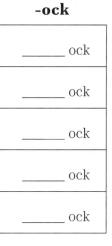

I will choose a group of onset cards with single consonants and consonant blends and place them, one at a time, in a pocket chart for the students to see. **Example:** *pr, cl, bl, l, r, s, v*

- As I place each onset in the chart, I will say the onset and then have students repeat after me.

- From the examples in the pocket chart, I will choose, or have the students help me to choose, the onset cards that will make a real word when paired with the *-ock* word family.

- Then, on the chart, I will write each appropriate consonant or consonant blend in the blank space in front of each rime, saying each onset followed by the rime and then having students repeat the onset and rime.

- As I fill in the blanks of the chart with the onsets, I will also identify objects in the room that contain the *-ock* word family. **Example:** *clock, block, sock, rock, lock*

- Using these words, or a selection of these words, I will create my own rhyme and share it with the children.

Guided Practice

I will be creating heterogeneous groups of two or three students. Each student will have a worksheet with five different word-family charts exactly like the one I modeled. Students will then work in their groups, selecting five cards from the onset deck and determining which onsets will make complete words when paired with any of the five word families. I will observe each group individually and monitor their progress. Some groups can work with all five word families at once, while other groups will need to focus on making words for one specific word family.

Independent Practice

Students will be able to fill in their word-family charts with real words they have come up with based on the selection of cards from the onset deck. Next, they will be asked to write at least two more words for each word family on their own.

Extended Practice

The students will use the information they have learned about the patterns of word families and onsets to write their own rhyme. The rhyme needs to include at least two different pairs of rhyming words. I would also like for the students to color code the onset with one color and the word family with a contrasting color.

Lesson Closing

The group will come back together, and those students who are finished will share their rhyme with the rest of the class. As a group, we will work together to identify the rhyming pairs, the onsets, and the word families. I will have for display a variety of books that contain these special word patterns so that students may enjoy more rhyming books.

Assessment and Evaluation

Assessment will be based on student perceptions throughout the lesson. Based on observation and interaction at the start of the lesson, I will determine which students have prior knowledge of rhyme, I will expect to see evidence of that in their written practice and formal assignment. Then I will use the checklist below to look for the following in their written assignment:

- At least two different pairs of rhyming words are used.
- Each pair of rhyming words contains the same word family.
- Correct color-coding of onset/consonant cluster.
- Correct color-coding of word family/rime.
- Correct spelling in the chosen word patterns.

In this chapter, we presented several instructional models for making poetry, rhymes, and songs an integral part of your daily instructional routine. The primary purpose of these instructional models is for students to learn to take aesthetic delight in the rhythm and language found in poetry, rhymes, and songs. A second purpose is to develop routines for mastery of important reading competencies.

These routines can form the basis for reading instruction that is effective in developing proficient readers and nurturing lifelong readers and language lovers. Again, feel free to adapt them to your own special circumstances. Be sure, however, that the elements mentioned at the beginning of this chapter continue to play a major role in your adaptation. And if you find that none of these models works well for you, feel empowered to use these routines as springboards to develop your own model of phonics and fluency instruction using rhyming poetry and songs as the core elements.

Chapter 4

Poetry and Word Study

In previous chapters, we pointed out and illustrated how using poetry, rhymes, and songs can help your students decode words. When teaching phonograms or word families to students, you can also teach word meanings through the rich meaningful context that surrounds the words in this genre. Learning to recognize words requires students to use all of the cue systems in written language—whole-word recognition, phonics, structural patterns, and context—which is essential to learning to read and achieving fluency (Heilman, Blair, & Rupley, 2002). Thus, a major task of teaching reading is to blend these instructional components properly for students' needs. Just because we add all the ingredients to bake a cake does not mean that we will have a tasty dessert. Merely adding the ingredients is meaningless, until they are blended together properly and baked with care. It is not until the chemistry of each ingredient becomes part of a whole, that a cake becomes greater than its individual parts. When words are recognized instantly, analysis is minimal. The reader can read fluently and focus on reading for meaning (Rasinski, Rupley & Nichols, 2009). Fluent reading and comprehension is the whole or the goal that we are aiming for through the use of poetry.

Word study should teach students not only to sound out words accurately but also to make associations and accommodations to their experiences and provide them with varied opportunities to practice, apply, and discuss their word knowledge in meaningful contexts. The ultimate goal of word study is for students to expand, refine, and add to their existing conceptual knowledge and to enhance their comprehension and understanding of what they read (Rupley, Logan & Nichols, 1999). The link between word-meaning knowledge (vocabulary) and comprehension is strong throughout students' education; insufficient word knowledge can often be the cause of differences in their comprehension capabilities. Students may be successful at decoding but can, and often do, struggle with comprehension when they encounter too many words for which they have limited or no meaning (Biemiller, 2003). A child's reading vocabulary is likely to increase at the rate of 3,000 to 4,000 words a year, resulting in a reading vocabulary of more than 25,000 words by eighth grade (Graves, 2006). Not having access to words that represent the concepts and content of what they read causes difficulty in students' comprehension of texts, limits their ability to make connections with their existing background knowledge, inhibits their capacity to make coherent inferences, and impacts their ability to reason. Moreover, vocabulary knowledge that is rich and well developed contributes significantly to fluent reading and writing.

Two Decoding Techniques

* *

Two effective word study techniques aimed primarily at decoding are applying consonant substitution until students can identify the unfamiliar word(s) and then combining known words to recognize and reveal their meaning. For example, when students learn words such as *cake* and *make* through poetry, they can then figure out the pronunciation and discuss the meaning of other words, such as *wake* and *lake*. You can also engage students in instruction to create and combine words to learn new words, such as *forsake* and *remake*. With this technique, you do not have to directly teach the sounds of the vowels, as the known word family or phonogram will naturally indicate the appropriate sound(s) and the context will help and support students to learn the words' meanings.

Word Harvesting

Word harvesting simply involves having students choose words that they think are interesting from a poem, displaying the words on a chart or other form of display, and then discussing the meaning and structure of the words. The words are put on display to prompt students (and you) to use them in oral and written language. Imagine if you read a new poem with your students every day and harvest five or six words from each new poem; by the end of a 180-day school year, students will have heard, read, chosen, and used 800–960 interesting and, most likely, new words to add to their vocabulary.

Additional activities can help students expand on the words they harvested for the word wall. For example, if *remote* was a harvested word, write it on the chart, then guide students in constructing two lists: one that contains words that are similar in meaning to the word *remote* and one that contains words that are opposite in meaning.

Example: *remote*

Similar	Different
distant	near
undiscovered	adjacent
inaccessible	close
isolated	occupied

Function Words From Poems

Because the activities we present throughout this book are based on words in context, numerous high-frequency words (e.g., *is, am, are,* and *that*) are also learned as units simply because students hear them and see them repeatedly in instruction using poetry, rhymes, and songs. Students' understanding of these structure words enable them to understand how they "glue our language together" and contribute to using syntax as a way of getting meaning from reading. Because students repeatedly see and read the words in rhyming poetry, they establish automatic stimulus-response patterns for dozens of high-frequency function words, such as *that*, *with*, *be*, *are*, *and*, *was*, *it*, *the*, *in*, *to*, *than*, *you*, *they*, *said*, *when*, and *can*. These words glue our language together and help us make sense in communication.

Function Word Deletion

To help students establish the concept that language must make sense and sound like language, you should present examples and have them think about and discuss language without these words. Focus your discussion and students' attention on how "funny" our language sounds without glue words, for example, by presenting this sentence: "Sam boy pole blond hair." Then add some glue words to show how much more meaningful and communicative the language becomes: "Sam is the boy by the pole with the blond hair." Once you feel that students have a grasp of the function of structure words, you can engage them in the activities described below.

Write a short poem on the board, deleting several function words.

BOWL SOUP

Table bowl soup eat / Bowl full meat
I eat bowl soup day / Bowl soup good I say

Discuss with students whether this poem makes sense. Does it sound like language? Then present the same poem to students with the glue words or function words included and see if it makes more sense to them.

THE BOWL OF SOUP

On the table is a bowl of soup to eat / This big bowl is full of meat
I eat a bowl of soup a day / This bowl of soup is good I must say

Your students will enjoy taking the structure words out of poems they have learned, exchanging them with a partner, and then reinserting the deleted words. You can have students cut apart the poems and rearrange the words, leaving out the glue words. Then have them write the glue words on strips of paper and insert these words into the poem as they reassemble it. For example, here is "The Purple Cow" from Chapter 2 without, and with, the structure words.

THE PURPLE COW

never Purple Cow,
never Hope See One;
tell, Anyhow,
I'd rather See One.

THE PURPLE COW

I never saw a Purple Cow,
I never Hope to See One;
But I can tell you, Anyhow,
I'd rather See than Be One.

Synonyms and Antonyms

One of the simplest and easiest ways to expand children's vocabularies is through the substitution of familiar words found in the poems and songs that they learn. The substitution of other words for the words they know makes for a powerful connector from one word to another. You can begin with something as simple as writing the following song on a strip of paper and expanding on it each day with words that are synonyms (sing to the tune of "Merrily We Roll Along"):

> This is the **doorway** to our room / To our room, to our room.
>
> This is the **doorway** to our room / That we come in each day.

Once students learn and sing this song, you can put a synonym over or under the word *doorway*.

> This is the **doorway** to our room / To our room, to our room.
> **(gateway)**
>
> This is the **doorway** to our room / That we come in each day
> **(gateway)**

Other words such as *entry, entryway, portal, access, entrance* can be used in the song.

To teach antonyms, substitute the highlighted words with words such as *outlet, exit,* and *exodus.*

> This is the **outlet** from our room / From our room, from our room.
>
> This is the **outlet** from our room / That we go out each day.

For a variation of this approach, use prepositions such as *under, beneath, below, underneath.* The following song is sung to the tune of "Oh Where, Oh Where Has My Little Dog Gone?"

> Oh where, oh where has my pencil gone / Oh where, oh where can it be?
>
> It's **under** your desk right there I see. / Oh would you please pick it up for me?

The variation below focuses on adjectives such as *tiny, diminutive,* and *small.*

> Oh where, oh where has my **tiny** pencil gone / Oh where, oh where can it be?
>
> With its **diminutive** size as small as a flea / I am afraid it is too **small** to see.

Because the text remains constant and you begin with familiar words that are in the children's vocabulary, they will learn to recognize and understand words such as *diminutive*.

Later, after children recognize and associate meaning with the words, the words can be randomly placed on a word wall. Leave a blank space for the object in the songs, so individual children can select a word to go in the blank space and place it where it should go. All the children can then sing the song and see if it makes sense with the chosen word.

Adding Illustrations

Pictures and illustrations can also be used to teach synonyms and antonyms in context and are especially effective when using rhymes that are easily constructed. For example, Bill Rupley wrote the poem below to teach synonyms for the word *big* using a picture of a cow. He wrote the poem on a flip chart and used a red marker (for the boldface words) to write the focus words. If you recall, we prefer a flip chart that keeps an ongoing record of actual activities that both you and your students can use again and again.

This cow is **big** as **big** can be

He is **huge** as we all can see

The cow is **jumbo** as a **jumbo** jet

He is so **large** we can't see around him yet

Yes, he is **sizeable**, that is for sure

His **enormous** size makes us all look miniature

Using antonyms for the same poem helps your students connect their knowledge of word meanings with a familiar activity. Here is the same poem featuring antonyms and an illustration of a small cow.

This cow is **small** as **small** can be

He is **tiny** as we all can see

The cow is **minute** as a **minute** ant

He is so **petite**, we can barely see him yet

Yes, he is **teeny**, that is for sure

His size makes him look **miniature**

Suggestions for Synonyms, Antonyms, and Combinations

Synonyms can include:

tall, large . . . (elevated, immense, soaring)

work, toil . . . (labor, function, job)

want, desire . . . (crave, prefer, hope)

Antonyms can include:

tall, large . . . (diminutive, petite, compact)

work, toil . . . (rest, recreation, sleep)

want, desire . . . (disgust, dislike, hate)

Combinations of meaning can include:

tall, petite . . . (elevated, compact, immense)

work, rest . . . (job, sleep, recreation)

want, need . . . (prefer, demand, require)

Games

As the synonym and antonym word wall grows and expands, you can introduce games to reinforce students' word learning.

WORDO

WORDO (Rasinski & Padak, 2007) is a simple game, yet one that students rarely tire of. Simply give each student a grid (3 x 3, 4 x 4, 5 x 5; a 4 x 4 grid is shown below). This will be their WORDO card. Have students randomly write a word from a selected list in each box.

WORDO is played like bingo. You call out a word, the definition of a word, or an illustrative sentence for a word. If a student has the word on a card, he or she covers the appropriate box with a marker. When a horizontal, vertical, or diagonal row of boxes are covered, the student calls out "WORDO!" After checking the card, you can award a small prize to the winner. Several rounds of WORDO can be played in a matter of minutes.

Missing Words

Missing Words is a variation of Jeopardy that works well with groups of students. Set up a pocket chart so that each column represents a category of synonyms (e.g., Entry Words, Position Words, Size Words, and so on). Each row represents a different value for the words (10, 20, 30, 40 points, and so on). One student from each group comes forward at a time to play. The student selects a category (a column) and value (a row). Present a sentence in which a targeted word has been deleted: *John came into our room through the p_____*. The first student to ring a bell has the opportunity to produce the missing word. If correct, the indicated point value is awarded to the team. If a student answers incorrectly, the students in the other groups are given an opportunity to produce the missing word.

Memory

This variation of Concentration involves students taking turns to match index cards containing words from a poem with index cards containing a definition or picture of that word. Cards are randomly placed face down in a grid to begin each game. If a match of word and definition is made, the student takes the two cards and play continues until all pairs are matched. If a match is not made, the cards are turned over and remain in place. The student who makes the most matches is the winner of the game.

Making Words

Pat and James Cunningham (1992; Rasinski & Zutell, 2010) created this anagram game for use particularly with struggling and developing readers and spellers. In Making Words, students work with a limited number of letters to build words *under the guidance of the teacher.* The fact that you guide students in the activity makes it something that developing and struggling readers will find beneficial.

Begin by determining a key word from a poem that you and your students have read. You will use its letters to make other words, so determine in advance all the words that can be made. The

Wordsmith Web site can do this for you in a matter of seconds: *www.wordsmith.org/anagram/ advanced.html* (click "Yes" to this question: *Show Candidate Word List Only?*).

From the letters in the word *hickory* (for a lesson done after reading "Hickory Dickory Dock"), the following words of two or more letters can be made:

rocky	rock	icky	cry	ho
choir	hick	icy	rho	or
Rick	cork	irk	coy	oh
hock	rich	chi	hi	yo

Then list the words you want to use in your lesson—this usually ranges from 6 to 15 words. Put the words in order, generally from the shortest or easiest to the longest or hardest. The final word in the lesson should be the word that contains all the letters (in the case above, *hickory* would be the final word). So for a group of first graders the words in the lesson might be *oh, ho, hi, cry, icy, icky, Rick, rock, rocky, hickory*.

Next, for each student, cut out (or have students cut out) squares from a sheet of paper or card stock and write one letter from the key word on each square (*h, i, c, k, o, r, y*). Vowels and consonants can be distinguished in some way (e.g., colors of the letters or the paper on which they are written). Give each student a set of letters. You should also have a large version of the letters and a pocket chart so you can do the lesson with your students and allow them to watch you manipulate your letters. The lesson is now ready to begin.

Simply guide your students to make words by arranging and rearranging the letters. As you and your students make the words, point out salient features of the words; for example, vowel and consonant sounds, vowel digraphs (*ee*), consonant blends (*st*), *r*-controlled vowels (*er*), number of syllables, and of course the essential meaning of each new word and an example of how it may be used in a sentence. Help students see how often one word is built from previous words, with just a small manipulation required as the sample below shows.

> *Boys and girls, take a vowel and consonant from the letter cards I gave you and make the word* oh, *as in an expression I like to use: "Oh, boy!"* (Students manipulate their letter cards to make the word. The teacher monitors their work, helping as needed, and makes the word, too, using large letter cards and the pocket chart.)
>
> *Now I'd like you to rearrange the letters to make a word that we often associate with Santa Claus.* (Students rearrange their letters to make *ho*.)
>
> *Now let's change one letter to make a word that we use when we greet or say hello to one another. What is that word?* (Students call out the word *hi*.)
>
> *That's correct. Make the word* hi.

The final word in each lesson is always the key word (sometimes called magic word, secret word, or challenge word). Again, it is the word that uses all the letters. For this last word, no clues are given initially. Students need to try to figure it out on their own. Knowing that the word is related to a poem that they recently read is usually enough for many students to figure this final word out. If students are unable to come up with the last word, you can give them the first and second letters and so on, or provide other clues that will allow them to be successful.

> *Now let's make one last word. It uses all the letters and is a word that we read in yesterday's poem.*

You can expand this lesson in several ways. First, you can find a letter pattern or two that you explored in the lesson and have students write new words using this pattern, and all the letters of the alphabet (A–Z). For example, from the hickory lesson, you could have students make these additional words: *-ick (lick, slick, pick, chick, stick, quick); -ory (story, glory, history).*

Once all your words are made, students can then sort them in various ways—by letter and sound pattern, number of syllables, number of letters, grammatical category, and so on. Words that students find interesting or unusual can also be added to the word wall for further practice and use.

Word Ladders

In Chapter 3, we introduced one of our favorite word study activities—word ladders! A word ladder is another word-building activity in which students change one letter in a word to make a new word (Beck, 2005; Rasinski, 2005, 2008; Rasinski & Zutell, 2010). Word families or phonograms are powerful tools for word recognition because they are rhyming word patterns that are found in many words in which one or two letters are changed. Because children's poems contain rhymes, they are treasure troves of word families. And so a natural extension of the reading and rereading of poetry is the completion of a word ladder that features the word families found in the poem.

For example, after reading "Star Light, Star Bright," you can lead your students in doing the following word ladder:

LIGHT: Change the first letter to make the opposite of *left*.

RIGHT: Change the first letter to make a word that means a *dispute*.

FIGHT: Change the first letter to make a word that means *power*.

MIGHT: Change the first letter to make another word for *vision*.

SIGHT: Subtract a letter to make a sound that you make when you are relieved.

SIGH: Change a letter to make the opposite of *low*.

HIGH

Although the word ladder may feel like a game to students, they are reinforcing their knowledge of the *-ight* and *-igh* word families and also expanding their vocabularies.

Increasing one's vocabulary (and ability to decode words) is much more than learning names to associate with experiences. Vocabulary knowledge closely reflects children's breadth of real-life and vicarious experiences. Students cannot comprehend and understand well without some knowledge of the concepts that are represented by the print. As noted by Rupley, Logan, and Nichols (1999), "Vocabulary is a shared component of reading and writing—it helps the author and the reader to comprehend through the shared meanings of words" (p. 337). We feel that poetry offers a rich contextual foundation for learning words. The activities in this chapter provide you with methods for building and expanding your students' word knowledge from that foundation.

Chapter 5

Extending the Poetry Experience:
Reading and Writing Poetry Parodies

Our experience has shown us that once children get into performing poetry, they want to write their own. And because of the brevity of most rhyming poetry for children, because of its rhythm and predictable structure, we have found that it is ideal for helping children, especially those who struggle with writing, to take a chance, have some fun with writing, and to set the stage for them to write even more.

Just as word families are a type of word-level linguistic pattern, rhyming poems themselves are one large linguistic pattern. Their rhyme and rhythmical pattern makes them easy to learn to read. Our brains detect the pattern, and after a few practice readings, most students are able to read such poems. The very same structure that makes rhyming poetry easy to read also makes it easy to emulate. We have found that students are naturally inclined to write their own poems based on the structure of the poems they have learned to read. We call this form of poetry "parody poems." How many of us have created our own versions of "Roses are red, violets are blue . . .?" And, when students begin to write their own parody poems, they develop even deeper understandings of the words they write and how those words are structured—and they have new material to read, reread, and perform for others. Moreover, by modeling their writing after an existing poem, students have the opportunity to write like the poet. The use of rhyming poetry creates the possibility of a circle of performance: students read poetry, they write poetry based on what they have read, and then they have new poetry (their own and their classmates') to read.

Moving Beyond Memorization

* *

We love using parody poems with students. Once students learn to read the original poem fluently, they quickly and easily memorize the text. However, once a text is memorized, students no longer have to track it visually, and when that happens, they are no longer reading. So at the point of memorization, we bring in some of the parodies that Bruce Lansky, Alan Katz, Rob Pottle, and other poets have written based on the original poem or lyric. When students read the parody, they are back to reading the text. The rhythm of the original poem is retained in the parody, and this makes learning the poem easy and enjoyable for students. However, the parody contains new words and ideas, so students have to read the text repeatedly in order to master it. This builds fluency. Moreover, since the parody also contains word families (e.g., the two parodies of "Yankee Doodle" in the next section contain the important -*ick* and -*ank* word families in multisyllabic words), students also have an opportunity to further develop their phonics skills. Parodies are wonderful texts to use in the instructional routines that we described in Chapter 3.

Parody Professionals

* *

Some professional poets are masters of writing parodies of familiar poems and song lyrics. In the previous section, we mentioned several of our favorites to use in the classroom. Bruce Lansky is one. Consider the following parodies that Lansky has written for the familiar song lyric, "Yankee Doodle."

YANKEE DOODLE

Yankee Doodle went to town
Riding on a chicken.
He went into a restaurant
And came out finger lickin'.

Yankee Doodle went to town
with his baby blankie.
Every time he blew his nose
he used it for a hankie.

Rob Pottle is another children's poet who is also a master of the parody. Many children are familiar with nursery rhymes such as "Wee Willie Winkie," and those who are not familiar with it can easily learn to read and recite this simple rhyme.

WEE WILLIE WINKIE

Wee Willie Winkie runs through the town,

Upstairs and downstairs in his nightgown,

Tapping at the window and crying through the lock,

Are all the children in their beds, it's past eight o'clock?

We read this text to our students while they follow along silently once or twice; then we read it chorally, once, twice, maybe even three times. Eventually, we allow individuals and small groups to perform it for the class. This is then followed by a short word lesson where we and the children point out interesting words for the word wall such as *tapping, nightgown, crying*. We also do the following: draw students' attention to the sound associated with the letter *W* as in *Wee, Willie,* and *Winkie*; notice the -*ing* ending in the words *crying* and *tapping*; and focus on the -*own*, -*ock*, and -*air* word families—charting words from the rhyme that contain these word families and adding other words, such as *frown, clown, dock, knock, rock, fair,* and *hair* to the display. In less than 15 minutes, we have implemented a reading lesson filled with authentic and engaging reading, followed by a high-powered and productive phonics lesson that covers several important phonics features.

On following days we take advantage of students' familiarity with the rhyme by doing similar lessons with these parodies that Rob Pottle created based on "Wee Willie Winkie."

WEE WILLIE STINKY *by Rob Pottle*

Wee Willie Stinky won't take a bath, / runs through the woods on a mountain path.
"Go, and take a shower," all the creatures say. / Skunks that get a whiff of him, turn and run away.

ANOTHER WEE WILLIE WINKIE *by Rob Pottle*

Wee Willie Winkie runs through the town, / Main Street, High Street, in a nightgown.
All the neighbors laughing, teasing him in jest. / Everybody starts to yell, "Go get dressed!"

With additional versions of "Wee Willie Winkie," Rob Pottle has provided us with enough material for students to have a ball practicing and performing poetry, feeling successful as readers, and learning plenty about the way that words work and what they mean. The same can be done with songs, another form of poetry.

After teaching children the song "You Are My Sunshine" using the Daily Poem Routine (see Chapter 3, pages 26–27), allow them to read and enjoy these Rob Pottle parodies:

YOU ARE MY TEACHER *by Rob Pottle*

You are my teacher. My favorite teacher. / You give me homework that takes all night.
And you ask questions that give me headaches. / It is rare that I get one right.

You are my teacher. My favorite teacher. / You give detentions to everyone.
And you make sure when we're in your classroom / nobody ever has fun.

You are my teacher. My favorite teacher. / I'm glad that you have so many rules.
I hope that you'll be my teacher next year. / And oh, by the way, April Fools.

YOU ARE MY STUDENT *by Rob Pottle*

You are my student. My favorite student. / You give me apples that have a worm.
And when I say to be still and quiet / You wiggle and giggle and squirm.

You are my student. My favorite student. / You never listen to what I say.
You don't do homework. You don't behave well. / You're always in trouble all day.

You are my student. My favorite student. / I'm really glad you ignore my rules.
I wish that all kids would act like you do. / And oh, by the way, April Fool's.

Alan Katz is another writer who also works with song lyrics. Here's his version of "Oh Susanna" that students love to read, reread, sing, and discover the interesting words and word parts used by the writer.

I'M SO CARSICK *by Alan Katz*

I'm in my dad's Toyota / And we're now in hour three
And we're gonna visit Grandma / Though I wish she'd drive to me.
We had some lunch / A while ago / A tiny pizza pie
I need a soda or some juice / 'Cause boy, my throat is dry!

I'm so carsick / Between you and me
We've been driving for so long that / I'm growing a goatee!
Some take the bus / Some take the train / And others get to fly
We're in this car, in the slow lane / I think I'm gonna cry!

I'm so carsick, / Gotta go wee-wee
Hey Dad, stop this Toyota / And next time, go without me!

The instant and natural motivation that comes from reading a funny text such as "I'm So Carsick" and "You Are My Teacher" makes students unaware that they are actually reading and developing critical reading skills.

Some parodies not only provide a vehicle for learning to read, they are also vehicles for learning actual content. Rob Pottle demonstrates this possibility with his parody of "Are You Sleeping?"

A TEST: LIST ALL FIFTY STATES *by Rob Pottle*

Minnesota,
North Dakota,
Idaho,
Ohio,
Washington, Alaska,
Oregon, Nebraska.
Forty-two
more it's true.

Alabama,
Indiana,
Michigan,
Maryland,
Maine and Mississippi,
I'm not yellin' "Yippie!"
'cause that's all
I recall.

Student-Authored Parodies

* *

If Bruce Lansky, Rob Pottle, Alan Katz, and other respected and successful writers can write parodies, students can as well. As we mentioned earlier, the rhythmical and rhyming pattern of the original poem makes it a template that helps students easily write (and then read, reread, and perform) their own poetry. Let's take another look at "Yankee Doodle." It has a very distinct rhythm and rhyme pattern. In fact, the pattern is so distinct and memorable that the song we sing today is really a parody of an old English folk tune that the British rewrote to mock the disheveled Americans who aided the British during the French and Indian War that preceded the Revolution. Although the song was used to poke fun at the American colonists, after a while, the Americans made the song their own, and before the end of the Revolution, wrote close to 200 patriotic versions of "Yankee Doodle." Here's one example:

> There was Captain Washington / Upon a slapping stallion
> A-giving orders to his men / I guess there was a million.

Given its distinct pattern, the easiest way to start a parody is simply by changing the second line of the lyric, the modifier to the first line. Lansky does this by having Yankee Doodle "riding on a chicken" and "with his baby blankie" (see page 48). Once the second line is developed, the writer needs to think of a rhyming word for the last word of the second line of each verse (*chicken* and *blankie*), and then write lines 3 and 4 that finish the thought and end with the rhyming word. Bruce chose *lickin'* and *hankie* as his two rhymes to finish his verses.

Can students do the same? Here are some parodies of "Yankee Doodle" written by elementary students, some of whom were struggling readers and writers enrolled in the reading clinic at Kent State University.

> Yankee Doodle went to town / Riding on a snail.
> "Wow, this ride is way too slow / I should have sent an email."

> Yankee Doodle went to town / Riding on a tugboat.
> The air was just a little brisk / So he put on his fur coat.

> Yankee Doodle went to town / Riding in a pickup truck.
> The truck got stuck in some muck. / And Yankee D was out of luck!

Of course, as students become more proficient in developing their own parodies, they will find that there are many other ways to create parodies. In the case of "Yankee Doodle," writers can change the main character, where the character is going, or any other part of the poem. One of our students swapped Wee Willie Winkie for Yankee Doodle to come up with another parody to "Yankee Doodle":

> Willie Winkie went to school / And met his brand new teacher.
> What a shock when he found out / His teacher was a creature!

Consider all the reading and writing that students could do with the variations of "Yankee Doodle" presented here! Five minutes of choral reading and singing of "Yankee Doodle" and parodies each morning for a month can add up to a lot reading and writing for your students!

In addition to "Yankee Doodle," many other poems, rhymes, and songs lend themselves to parody. Again, the rhythmical nature of any rhyming poem gives it a structure that is easy to replicate. Here are a few examples written (practiced and later performed) by students in the Kent State University reading clinic.

ORIGINAL

Jack and Jill ran up the hill
To fetch a pail of water.
Jack fell down and broke his crown
And Jill came tumbling after.

PARODY

Jane and Jack attacked a stack
Of hot blueberry pancakes.
The cakes fought back, then Jane and Jack
Went straight to bed with tummy aches.

ORIGINAL

Diddle, diddle, dumpling, my son John
Went to bed with his stockings on;
One shoe off, and one shoe on
Diddle, diddle, diddle, dumpling,
     my son John.

PARODIES

Diddle, diddle, dumpling, my son Mike
Loves to ride on his two wheel bike;
Got a flat tire, and had to hike
Diddle, diddle, dumpling, my son Mike.

Fiddle, faddle, fuddle, my friend Fred
Went to the doctor and she sent him to bed;
Now chicken soup is all that he's fed
Fiddle, faddle, fuddle, my friend Fred.

ORIGINAL

Hickory, dickory, dock,
The mouse ran up the clock.
The clock struck one,
The mouse ran down,
Hickory, dickory, dock.

PARODIES

Hickory, dickory, dock, / The bird flew into the clock.
The clock struck three, / She sang with glee,
Hickory, dickory, dock.

Hickory, dickory, dack, / The duck flew into my shack.
The duck did quack, / He flew out the back,
Hickory dickory dack.

Hickory, smickory, smack, / I'm hungry for a snack.
Some crackers and cheese, / Can I have some please?
Hickory, smickory, smack.

Poet David Harrison wrote this version of "Old MacDonald" so that teachers and students could develop their own personal verses to the song:

Ms. McDonald has a class, oh my oh my oh,
And in her class is Laughing Lil, oh my oh my oh,
With a "ha-ha" here and a "ha-ha" there / Here a "ha" there a "ha" / Everywhere a "ha-ha"
Ms. McDonald has a class, oh my oh my oh.

Ms. McDonald has a class, oh my oh my oh,
And in her class is Sniffing Sam, oh my oh my oh,
With a "sniff, sniff" here and a "sniff, sniff" there
Here a "sniff" there a "sniff" / Everywhere a "sniff, sniff"
"Ha-ha" here and a "ha-ha" there / Here a "ha" there a "ha" / Everywhere a "ha-ha"
Ms. McDonald has a class, oh my oh my oh.

Ms. McDonald has a class, oh my oh my oh, / And in her class is Wiggly Will, oh my oh my oh,
With a "wiggle, wiggle" here and a "wiggle, wiggle" there
Here a "wiggle" there a "wiggle" / Everywhere a "wiggle, wiggle"
"Sniff, sniff" here and a "sniff, sniff" there / Here a "sniff" there a "sniff" / Everywhere a "sniff, sniff"
"Ha-ha" here and a "ha-ha" there / Here a "ha" there a "ha" / Everywhere a "ha-ha"
Ms. McDonald has a class, oh my oh my oh.

These examples demonstrate how the parodies that students write can go from the simple alterations of the original to parodies that, although they contain the same rhythmical structure as the original, have text that is quite different from the original.

Writing parodies does not take a lot of time. Once students discover the pattern, it is often a matter of filling in the blanks. However, when the process of parody writing becomes a regular instructional routine, students develop greater sophistication in their ability to write them. Writing becomes more than filling in the blanks as students tell their own story through their poem.

Moreover, writing parodies as a regular instructional routine will help students develop a better sense of the role of rhythm in language, make them better able to detect and use rhymes, and of course, become more sensitive to finding just the right words to make a poem work well. All this builds proficiency in writing and phonics. And since you will ask students to perform their own and their classmates' poems, rehearsal will also become part of the process, and proficiency in fluency will also increase.

Finally, poetry is meant to be shared with an audience, either orally or in print. Poetry can also be shared through publication. With the new technology available for making books, it is a fairly simple task to transform the poems (including parodies) written by your students into books that you can give to students and parents to enjoy at home and also to put into the classroom and school libraries for further reading.

At the Kent State University Reading Clinic, students regularly write poetry, mostly parodies. Toward the end of the clinic period, students submit two or three of their best poems. We

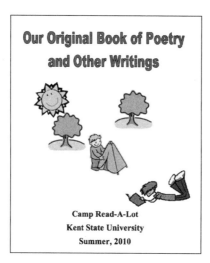

turn these individual poems into poetry collections in book form and present them to students and their parents at the end of the clinic. The look on the children's faces tells us that being a published poet is something special. Parents tell us that at home, the poetry in the books is read and reread by students and their family members. In fact, Tim has received numerous calls from parents asking for additional copies of their children's poetry books, some to replace the books on the coffee table at home that have been read so often that the pages have worn out, and some to put into children's scrapbooks as a reminder of their success and the fun they had learning to read in a summer reading program for struggling readers!

Teaching Students to Write Parodies

* *

In Chapter 3, we provide models for using rhyming poetry in the classroom for reading. These lesson formats are easily adapted to student-written parodies. Once students are acquainted with the routine of practicing and eventually performing poetry that others have written, you can ask them to take their chosen poem and write their own version.

You may want to begin with a common classroom poem and have each student (or pair of students) write a parody of the same poem. Follow this process:

- Begin by walking students through the structure of the poem (recall how we presented "Yankee Doodle" on page 51), share some examples that others have written in the past, and walk students through your own development of a parody.

- Then, as a class, work together to create a class-authored version of the selected poem.

- Once students feel more comfortable with the process, invite them to write their own parody, or work with a partner to create a poem.

At first, the process will feel clunky. We all feel anxious when we are asked to do something that is new and outside of our comfort zone. However, if you do this on a regular basis, you will find that your students soon become experts at writing their own poetry parodies. And, of course, as students become even more adept at writing more sophisticated parodies, they will eventually reach the point where they will be able to write their own original poetry.

Good teaching begins with you, the teacher, taking primary responsibility for the task to be learned. Over time, however, responsibility is gradually handed over to students and your support is gradually withdrawn. This model of poetry writing is, we feel, an exemplary model of how good teaching happens: Responsibility shifts from teacher to students, and support is gently removed. Eventually, students become independent in their ability to do the task.

A Matter of Scaffolding and Support

* *

Younger and struggling readers need all the support they can get in becoming successful as readers and writers. Normally, we provide the support for students by building background, previewing challenging words, and reading with them, as in assisted reading. Sometimes, however, we can find texts that, by their very nature, provide deep support for students. Rhyming poetry is one of these texts. In this book, we have made the case that rhyming poetry can support reading through its brevity, structure, use of rhyme, and its inherent invitation for practice or rehearsal. Similarly, rhyming poetry provides a wonderful scaffold for students to emerge as writers of poetry. The same brevity, structure, and rhyme that support readers can be used to support children in developing as writers—writers whose texts can be celebrated through performance and publication!

Visit these Web sites to find song lyrics, parody poems, and poems that students can rewrite as parodies:

Parodies, Songs, and Poems

David Harrison: *mowrites4kids.drury.edu/authors/harrison*

Brod Bagert: *brodbagert.com*

Bruce Lansky: *gigglepoetry.com*

Kenn Nesbitt: *www.poetry4kids.com*

Ted Scheu: *www.poetryguy.com*

Darren Sardelli: *www.laughalotpoetry.com*

Eric Ode: *www.ericode.com/index.htm*

Robert Pottle: *www.robertpottle.com*

Linda Knaus: *www.lindaknaus.com/index2.htm*

www.funnypoets.com

www.storyit.com/Classics/JustPoems/index.htm

bussongs.com

kidsmusictown.com/childrenssongslyrics/nurseryrhymes

www.rhymes.org.uk

www.lanterntree.com/nurseryrhymes/nurseryrhymeindex.html

www.smart-central.com

www.theteachersguide.com/ChildrensSongs.htm

www.kididdles.com/lyrics/allsongs.html

kids.niehs.nih.gov/music.htm

Rhyming Poetry and Song Books

Books by Brod Bagert

Giant Children (Dial Books, 2002)
Rainbows, Head Lice, and Pea-Green Tile: Poems in the Voice of the Classroom Teacher (Maupin House, 1999)
Shout! Little Poems that Roar (Dial Books, 2007)
School Fever (Dial Books, 2008)
Chicken Socks: And Other Contagious Poems (Boyds Mills Press, 1994)
Let Me Be the Boss: Poems for Kids to Perform (Boyds Mills Press, 1992)
The Gooch Machine: Poems for Children to Perform (Boyds Mills Press, 1997)

Books by David Harrison

Vacation, We're Going to the Ocean! (Boyds Mills Press, 2009)
Pirates (Boyds Mills Press, 2008)
Bugs: Poems About Creeping Things (Boyds Mills Press, 2007)
Sounds of Rain (Boyds Mills Press, 2006)
Farmer's Dog Goes to the Forest (Boyds Mills Press, 2005)
Connecting Dots: Poems of My Journey (Boyds Mills Press, 2004)
The Mouse Was Out at Recess (Boyds Mills Press, 2003)
The Alligator in the Closet (Boyds Mills Press, 2003)
Farmer's Garden (Boyds Mills Press, 2000)
Wild Country (Boyds Mills Press, 1999)
The Purchase of Small Secrets (Boyds Mills Press, 1998)
A Thousand Cousins (Boyds Mills Press, 1996)
The Boy Who Counted Stars (Boyds Mills Press, 1994)
Somebody Catch My Homework (Boyds Mills Press, 1993)
Partner Poems for Building Fluency: 40 Two-Voice Poems With Motivating Activities That Help Students Improve Their Fluency and Comprehension (with Rasinski, Timothy; Harrison, David L.; and Fawcett, Gay: Scholastic, 2009)

Books by Alan Katz

Take Me Out of the Bathtub and Other Silly Dilly Songs (Margaret K. McElderry, 2001)
On Top of the Potty: And Other Get-Up-and-Go Songs (Margaret K. McElderry, 2008)
Are You Quite Polite? Silly Dilly Manners Songs (Margaret K. McElderry, 2006)
I'm Still Here in the Bathtub: Brand New Silly Dilly Songs (Margaret K. McElderry, 2003)
Smelly Locker: Silly Dilly School Songs (Margaret K. McElderry, 2008)
Too Much Kissing! And Other Silly Dilly Songs About Parents (Margaret K. McElderry, 2009)
Going, Going, Gone! And Other Silly Dilly Sports Songs (Margaret K. McElderry, 2009)
Where Did They Hide My Presents? Silly Dilly Christmas Songs (Margaret K. McElderry, 2005)

Books by Bruce Lansky

Kids Pick the Funniest Poems (Meadowbrook, 1991)
I've Been Burping in the Classroom (Meadowbrook, 2007)
If Kids Ruled the School (Meadowbrook, 2004)

Mary Had a Little Jam (Meadowbrook, 2004)
No More Homework, No More Tests (Meadowbrook, 1997)
Oh My Darling, Porcupine (Meadowbrook, 2009)

Books by Robert Pottle

I'm Allergic to School (Meadowbrook, 2007)
Poems With Moxie (Blue Lobster Press, 2008)

Chapter 6

Collecting Poetry for Teaching Reading

Poetry, songs, and rhymes take readers to new heights, introduce them to new worlds, amuse them with humorous insights, tickle their funny bones, touch their sensitivity, and connect them with others. Poetry, song lyrics, and rhymes can increase students' awareness of language and exercise their minds as they connect and reconnect with the text in new ways. We feel that poetry, songs, and rhymes are effective instructional materials for teachers to use when teaching reading. They can help students succeed at learning on a daily basis and enhance their capabilities to read, write, and think critically (Burkhardt, 2006). According to Drew and Connor (1961):

> *The basic nature and function of poetry remains the same in all ages: it is to recreate the living truth of individual human experience through the medium of patterned language. Like the other arts, poetry brings form and order out of the confusion and discord of the living of life.* (p. 2)

Over the many years that we have been involved in reading clinics, tutoring services, and working with classroom teachers, we have accumulated nursery rhymes, rhyming poetry, song lyrics, and other forms of poetry to work with readers of all ability types and dispositions toward reading. More recently, we have been working alongside classroom teachers in an attempt to collect rhyming poetry and other text sources that can easily be aligned with word-family activities, are fun to read, and have many possibilities in regard to interpretation and performance. In this chapter, we share some of those collections with you, as well as some Web-based resources that you may find helpful in locating poems for themes, word families, or the multiple reading levels that each classroom teacher encounters.

For the most part over the years, we have used nursery rhymes and Mother Goose collections because they are very accessible, are in the public domain, and are just fun to read. We have had great success with a variety of nursery rhymes ranging from short, simple poems to longer, more involved poems. In addition, as we have worked with a wide variety of learners over the years, we have also added lengthier poems for continued fluency development, as well as for increasing opportunities for readers theater activities. The ones that we share here are just the beginning.

There are so many resources currently available to teachers that all one has to do is Google "poems and rhymes for kids" and you will have more resources than you know what to do with!

As we've discussed throughout this book, poetry that contains rhymes often exposes children to common word families. One way that we have assisted teachers over the years is to help them identify such poetry. Once you familiarize yourself with common word families, such as Edward Fry's most common phonograms, locating poetry to use in the classroom is quite simple. We encourage you to begin collecting poems around word families and other themes so you will have them readily available to teach. Several of the schools we have worked with have amassed vast collections of poems that have been sorted by reading levels, word families, and other categories or themes, such as holidays, seasons, cultures, humor, and so on.

Recently a wonderful teacher, Trish Mincey, shared with Dee three magazines called *The Grade Teacher* written in 1949 and 1950 as she knew we were working on this chapter. It was a lot of fun to look through these "Professional Magazines for Classroom Teachers of All Grades" as they were loaded with many ideas and resources, not to mention great ads and fashion advice for teachers! The primary reason Trish shared these teacher magazines with Dee is that they included poems, songs, and recommended recitations for the primary grades. Each text was developed around a theme and included plenty of word families.

The point of this vignette is that, as any reading researcher and teacher will tell you, what we are proposing in this book is not radical, new, or innovative. The idea of using poetry and music to help young readers develop reading skills and fluency has been around for years. We are delighted to share some ideas, thoughts, and poems with you and hope you will find these resources useful.

Poems for Teaching Selected Word Families

* *

First, we will present poems categorized by word families, starting with simple and short nursery rhymes, and then we will move to more complex, lengthier poems that also share common word families and vowel patterns. Finally, we will conclude with some poems organized around other themes and disperse some Web resources as we go. The following poems have all been selected because they contain common word families worth teaching to children. We start each section with a list of word families that will be encountered in the poem. Each list begins with boldface words that are found in the poem. Under each, we list other words from the poem and add a few other words that share the same word family. While there are often many word families contained in each poem, we have selected just a few from each poem. (Again, for examples and frameworks for using rhyming poetry and songs in your classroom, see Chapter 3.)

Word Families for the Word Wall for "Hush-a-Bye, Baby"

fall	**treetop**	**rock**
ball tall call wall small hall	pop cop hop mop stop drop	sock lock block clock knock

HUSH-A-BYE, BABY *Mother Goose*

Hush-a-bye, baby, on the treetop,

When the wind blows, the cradle will rock;

When the bough breaks, the cradle will fall;

Down will come baby, and cradle, and all!

Word Families for the Word Wall for "The Dog"

shove	test	
love dove above	best rest crest west	lovingest pest

THE DOG *by Ogden Nash*

The truth I do not stretch or shove

When I state the dog is full of love.

I've also proved, by actual test,

A wet dog is the lovingest.

Word Families for the Word Wall for "A Fly and a Flea in a Flue"

flue	do	flee
glue blue true	to who too boo zoo	tree bee tee see three

A FLY AND A FLEA IN A FLUE *by Anonymous*

A Fly and a Flea in a Flue / Were imprisoned, so what could they do?

Said the fly, "Let us flee!" / "Let us fly!" said the flea,

And they flew through a flaw in the flue.

Word Families for the Word Wall for "I'm Nobody"

frog			too		
dog	hog	logger	coo	achoo	kangaroo
log	fog	bog	boo	zoo	

I'M NOBODY *by Emily Dickinson*

I'm nobody! Who are you?

Are you nobody, too?

Then there's a pair of us—don't tell!

They'd banish us, you know.

How dreary to be somebody!

How public like a frog

To tell your name the livelong day

To an admiring bog!

Word Families for the Word Wall for "Motto for a Dog"

paws		dark	
claw	saw	bark	shark
law	draw	spark	lark
		spark	hark

MOTTO FOR A DOG *by Arthur Guiterman*

I love this little house because

It offers after dark,

A pause for rest, a rest for paws,

A place to moor my bark.

Word Families for the Word Wall for "There Was a Young Maid Who Said, 'Why'"

why	it				
try cry my fly	hit	kit	sit	fit	pit
	wit	quit	knit	bit	

THERE WAS A YOUNG MAID WHO SAID, "WHY"

There was a young maid who said, "Why
Can't I look in my ear with my eye?
If I give my mind to it,
I'm sure I can do it,
You never can tell till you try."

Word Families for the Word Wall for "'Bow Wow,' Says the Dog"

dog	cat	duck	crow
hog bog	rat sat	stuck truck	row throw know
frog clog	pat mat	pluck tuck	tow flow snow
fog	flat	muck yuck	sparrow

"BOW WOW," SAYS THE DOG *Mother Goose*

"Bow, wow,"
says the dog;
"Mew, mew,"
says the cat.
"Grunt, grunt,"
goes the hog;
And "squeak,"
goes the rat.

"Chirp, chirp,"
says the sparrow;
"Caw, caw,"
says the crow.
"Quack, quack,"
says the duck;
And what the cuckoos say,
you know.

For More Advanced Readers

The next few examples of rhyming poetry are for the more advanced readers who desire a challenge and are already beginning to develop fluency, but who need continued practice.

Words for the Word Family Wall Associated With "The Hayloft"

side	crops	play	nail	dwell
wide hide	tops stops	hay stay	mail pail	tell shell
tide ride	hops shops	day clay	tail rail	well fell
	mops pops	may pray	trail flail	smell
		way	wail fail	

THE HAYLOFT *by Robert Louis Stevenson*

Through all the pleasant meadow-side / The grass grew shoulder-high,
Till the shining scythes went far and wide / And cut it down to dry.

Those green and sweetly smelling crops / They led in wagons home;
And they piled them here in mountain tops / For mountaineers to roam.

Here is Mount Clear, Mount Rusty-Nail / Mount Eagle and Mount High—
The mice that in these mountains dwell, / No happier are than I!

Oh, what a joy to clamber there, / Oh, what a place for play,
With the sweet, the dim, the dusty air, / The happy hills of hay!

Word Families for the Word Wall for "The Cricket"

away	fast	run	tug	me
play may way	last past	sun gun	bug dug	he be
lay pay clay	mast cast	pun nun	shrug pug	see tree
stay stray day	vast	shun fun	lug plug	she we
say		spun		bee

THE CRICKET *by Marjorie Barrows*

And when the rain had gone away / And it was shining everywhere,
I ran out on the walk to play / And found a little bug was there.
And he was running just as fast / As any little bug could run,
Until he stopped for breath at last, / All black and shiny in the sun.

And then he chirped a song to me / And gave his wings a little tug,
And that's the way he showed that he / Was very glad to be a bug!

Longer Nursery Rhymes With
Selected Word Families

* *

Words for the Word Family Wall Associated With "A Nonsense Rhyme"

jing	krung	pent	morass	alack	strain	brow
sing	plung	went	grass	back	refrain	how
thing	sung	spent	pass	lack	rain	cow
spring	upflung	rent	mass	sack	main	wow
cling	unsung	tent	lass	pack	pain	plow
sting	unstrung	vent	crass	tack	train	bow
string	rung	lent	class	track	plain	chow
ring	flung	relentless		crack	stain	
wing	stung	scent		black		
king	hung			shack		
ding						
fling						

A NONSENSE RHYME *by James Whitcomb Riley*

Ringlety-jing!
And what will we sing?
Some little crinkety-crankety thing

That rhymes and chimes,

And skips, sometimes,

As though wound up with a kink in the spring.

Grunkety-krung

And chunkety-plung!

Sing the song that the bullfrog sung,—

A song of the soul

Of a mad tadpole

That met his fate in a leaky bowl;

And it's O for the first false wiggle he made

In a sea of pale pink lemonade!

And it's O for the thirst

Within him pent,

And the hopes that burst

As his reason went—

When his strong arm failed and his strength was spent!

Sing, O sing

Of the things that cling,

And the claws that clutch and the fangs that sting—

Till the tadpole's tongue

And his tail upflung

Quavered and failed with a song unsung!

O the dank despair in the rank morass,

Where the crawfish crouch in the cringing grass,

And the long limp rune of the loon wails on

For the mad, sad soul

Of a bad tadpole

Forever lost and gone!

Jinglety-jee!

And now we'll see

What the last of the lay shall be,

As the dismal tip of the tune, O friends,

Swoons away and the long tail ends.

And it's O, and alack!

For the tangled legs

 Phonics & Fluency Practice With Poetry © 2012 by Rasinski, Rupley, & Nichols • Scholastic Teaching Resources

And the spangled back
Of the green grig's eggs,
And the unstrung strain
Of the strange refrain
That the winds wind up like a strand of rain!

And it's O,
Also,
For the ears wreathed low,
Like a laurel wreath on the lifted brow
Of the frog that chants of the why and how,
And the wherefore too, and the thus and so
Of the wail he weaves in a woof of woe!
Twangle, then, with your wrangling strings,
The tinkling links of a thousand things!
And clang the pang of a maddening moan
Till the Echo, hid in a land unknown,
Shall leap as he hears, and hoot and hoo
Like the wretched wraith of a Whoopty-Doo!

Seasonal Poems With Selected Word Families

* *

Many schools as well as families celebrate the changing of the seasons, and the holidays and events that come along with them. We have included a sample of a poem that could be used in the fall around Halloween. We have also included some links at the end of this chapter where teachers can find other poems to celebrate the seasons.

Word Families for the Word Wall for "Black and Gold"

gold	tonight	black	ink
hold fold	candlelight	back pack	blinking blink
mold told	night light	sack tack	think stink
old cold	fight right	track rack	shrink link
sold	plight firelight		

BLACK AND GOLD *by Nancy Byrd Turner*

Everything is black and gold, / Black and gold, tonight:

Yellow pumpkins, yellow moon, / Yellow candlelight;

Jet-black cat with golden eyes, / Shadows black as ink,

Firelight blinking in the dark / With a yellow blink.

Black and gold, black and gold, / Nothing in between—

When the world turns black and gold, / Then it's Halloween!

Longer Poems for Upper Elementary Students

* *

The poems in this section are intended for upper elementary learners, who can still benefit from word family and fluency instruction, while also working on vocabulary development and enrichment activities. These poems provide great examples of the power of language and word choice and have the appropriate amount of text for repeated and partner readings.

THE BROOK *by Alfred Tennyson*

I come from haunts of coot and hern, / I make a sudden sally,
And sparkle out among the fern, / To bicker down a valley.

By thirty hills I hurry down, / Or slip between the ridges,
By twenty thorpes, a little town, / And half a hundred bridges.

Till last by Philip's farm I flow / To join the brimming river,
For men may come and men may go, / But I go on forever.

I chatter over stony ways, / In little sharps and trebles,
I bubble into eddying bays, / I babble on the pebbles.

With many a curve my banks I fret / By many a field and fallow,
And many a fairy foreland set / With willow-weed and mallow.

I chatter, chatter, as I flow / To join the brimming river,
For men may come and men may go, / But I go on forever.

I wind about, and in and out, / With here a blossom sailing,
And here and there a lusty trout, / And here and there a grayling,

And here and there a foamy flake / Upon me, as I travel
With many a silvery water-break / Above the golden gravel,

And draw them all along, and flow / To join the brimming river,
For men may come and men may go, / But I go on forever.

I steal by lawns and grassy plots, / I slide by hazel covers;
I move the sweet forget-me-nots / That grow for happy lovers.

I slip, I slide, I gloom, I glance, / Among the skimming swallows;
I make the netted sunbeam dance / Against my sandy shallows.

I murmur under moon and stars / In brambly wilderness;
I linger by my shingly bars; / I loiter round my cresses;

And out again I curve and flow / To join the brimming river,
For men may come and men may go, / But I go on forever.

THE TYGER *by William Blake*

Tyger, tyger, burning bright, / In the forests of the night,
What immortal hand or eye, / Could frame thy fearful symmetry?

In what distant deeps or skies / Burnt the fire of thine eyes?
On what wings dare he aspire? / What the hand dare seize the fire?

And what shoulder, and what art, / Could twist the sinews of thy heart?
And, when thy heart began to beat, / What dread hand, and what dread feet?

What the hammer? what the chain? / In what furnace was thy brain?
What the anvil? what dread grasp / Dare its deadly terrors clasp?

When the stars threw down their spears, / And watered heaven with their tears,
Did He smile His work to see? / Did He who made the lamb make thee?

Tyger, tyger, burning bright / In the forests of the night,
What immortal hand or eye, / Dare frame thy fearful symmetry?

FIRE AND ICE *by Robert Frost*

Some say the world will end in fire,
Some say in ice.
From what I've tasted of desire
I hold with those who favor fire.

But if it had to perish twice,
I think I know enough of hate
To say that for destruction ice
Is also great
And would suffice.

Using Poems for Readers Theater

Poems such as "Paul Revere's Ride" can easily be transformed into readers theater activities for increasing students' fluency. It is also easy to find word families within this poem for continued phonics reinforcement activities.

PAUL REVERE'S RIDE

by Henry Wadsworth Longfellow

Listen, my children, and you shall hear
Of the midnight ride of Paul Revere,
On the eighteenth of April, in Seventy-five;
Hardly a man is now alive
Who remembers that famous day and year.

He said to his friend, "If the British march
By land or sea from the town tonight,
Hang a lantern aloft in the belfry arch
Of the North Church tower as a signal light,—
One, if by land, and two, if by sea;
And I on the opposite shore will be,
Ready to ride and spread the alarm
Through every Middlesex village and farm,
For the country folk to be up and to arm."
Then he said, "Good-night!" and with muffled oar
Silently rowed to the Charlestown shore,
Just as the moon rose over the bay,
Where swinging wide at her moorings lay

The Somerset, British man-of-war;
A phantom ship, with each mast and spar
Across the moon like a prison bar,
And a huge black hulk, that was magnified
By its own reflection in the tide.

Meanwhile, his friend, through alley and street,
Wanders and watches with eager ears,
Till in the silence around him he hears
The muster of men at the barrack door,
The sound of arms, and the tramp of feet,
And the measured tread of the grenadiers,
Marching down to their boats on the shore.

Then he climbed the tower of the Old North Church,
By the wooden stairs, with stealthy tread,
To the belfry-chamber overhead,
And startled the pigeons from their perch
On the somber rafters, that round him made
Masses and moving shapes of shade,—
By the trembling ladder, steep and tall,
To the highest window in the wall,
Where he paused to listen and look down
A moment on the roofs of the town,
And the moonlight flowing over all.
Beneath, in the churchyard, lay the dead,
In their night-encampment on the hill,
Wrapped in silence so deep and still
That he could hear, like a sentinel's tread,
The watchful night-wind, as it went
Creeping along from tent to tent,
And seeming to whisper, "All is well!"
A moment only he feels the spell
Of the place and the hour, and the secret dread
Of the lonely belfry and the dead;
For suddenly all his thoughts are bent

On a shadowy something far away,
Where the river widens to meet the bay,—
A line of black that bends and floats
On the rising tide, like a bridge of boats.

Meanwhile, impatient to mount and ride,
Booted and spurred, with a heavy stride
On the opposite shore walked Paul Revere.
Now he patted his horse's side,
Now gazed at the landscape far and near,
Then, impetuous, stamped the earth,
And turned and tightened his saddle girth;
But mostly he watched with eager search
The belfry-tower of the Old North Church,
As it rose above the graves on the hill,
Lonely and spectral and somber and still.
And lo! As he looks, on the belfry's height
A glimmer, and then a gleam of light!
He springs to the saddle, the bridle he turns,
But lingers and gazes, till full on his sight,
A second lamp in the belfry burns!
A hurry of hoofs in the village street,
A shape in the moonlight, a bulk in the dark,
And beneath, from the pebbles, in passing, a spark
Struck out by a steed flying fearless and fleet:
That was all! And yet, through the gloom and the light,
The fate of a nation was riding that night;
And the spark struck out by that steed, in his flight,
Kindled the land into flame with its heat.
He has left the village and mounted the steep,
And beneath him, tranquil and broad and deep,
Is the Mystic, meeting the ocean tides;
And under the alders that skirt its edge,
Now soft on the sand, now loud on the ledge,
Is heard the tramp of his steed as he rides.

 Phonics & Fluency Practice With Poetry © 2012 by Rasinski, Rupley, & Nichols • Scholastic Teaching Resources

It was twelve by the village clock,
When he crossed the bridge into Medford town.
He heard the crowing of the cock,
And the barking of the farmer's dog,
And felt the damp of the river fog,
That rises after the sun goes down.

It was one by the village clock,
When he galloped into Lexington.
He saw the gilded weathercock
Swim in the moonlight as he passed,
And the meeting-house windows, blank and bare,
Gaze at him with a spectral glare,
As if they already stood aghast
At the bloody work they would look upon.

It was two by the village clock,
When he came to the bridge in Concord town.
He heard the bleating of the flock,
And the twitter of birds among the trees,
And felt the breath of the morning breeze
Blowing over the meadows brown.
And one was safe and asleep in his bed
Who at the bridge would be first to fall,
Who that day would be lying dead,
Pierced by a British musket-ball.

You know the rest. In the books you have read,
How the British Regulars fired and fled,—
How the farmers gave them ball for ball,
From behind each fence and farm-yard wall,
Chasing the red-coats down the lane,
Then crossing the fields to emerge again
Under the trees at the turn of the road,
And only pausing to fire and load.

So through the night rode Paul Revere;
And so through the night went his cry of alarm

To every Middlesex village and farm,—
A cry of defiance and not of fear,
A voice in the darkness, a knock at the door,
And a word that shall echo forevermore!
For, borne on the night-wind of the Past,
Through all our history, to the last,
In the hour of darkness and peril and need,
The people will waken and listen to hear
The hurrying hoof-beats of that steed
And the midnight message of Paul Revere.

Rhyming Songs for Fluency Practice That Includes Word Families

* * * * * * * * * * * * * * * * * * * *

As demonstrated in Chapter 5, this song, and others, can easily be converted into a variety of parodies.

YANKEE DOODLE

Father and I went down to camp,
Along with Captain Gooding,
And there we saw the men and boys
As thick as hasty puddin'.

Yankee Doodle keep it up,
Yankee Doodle dandy,
Mind the music and the step,
And with the girls be handy.

And there was Captain Washington,
Upon a slapping stallion,
And giving orders to his men,
I guess there was a million.

Yankee Doodle keep it up,
Yankee Doodle dandy,
Mind the music and the step,
And with the girls be handy.

And then the feathers on his hat,
They looked so' tarnal fin-a
I wanted pockily to get,
To give to my Jemina.

Yankee Doodle keep it up,
Yankee Doodle dandy,
Mind the music and the step,
And with the girls be handy.

And then we saw a swamping gun,
Large as a log of maple,
Upon a deuced little cart,
A load for father's cattle.

Yankee Doodle keep it up,
Yankee Doodle dandy,
Mind the music and the step,
And with the girls be handy.

THANKSGIVING DAY *by Lydia Maria Child*

Over the river and through the wood,
To grandfather's house we go;
The horse knows the way
To carry the sleigh
Through the white and drifted snow.

Over the river and through the wood—
Oh, how the wind does blow!
It stings the toes
And bites the nose,
As over the ground we go.

Over the river and through the wood,
To have a first-rate play.
Hear the bells ring,
"Ting-a-ling-ding!"
Hurrah for Thanksgiving Day!

Over the river and through the wood
Trot fast, my dapple gray!
Spring over the ground,
Like a hunting-hound!
For this is Thanksgiving Day.

Over the river and through the wood,
And straight through the barnyard gate.
We seem to go
Extremely slow,—
It is so hard to wait!

Over the river and through the wood,—
Now grandmother's cap I spy!
Hurrah for the fun!
Is the pudding done?
Hurrah for the pumpkin pie!

Poetry as a Connection to the World

As we previously stated, poetry provides powerful examples of the uses of language. Common literary elements in poems include the use of metaphor, simile, rhyme, and imagery, which we feel has a strong impact on our innermost selves, making poetry something that can be shared throughout our lives. The cultural heritage of the world has a rich and abundant history with poetry, and we can learn much about ourselves and the rest of the world as we investigate themes and topics that universally connect us. Poetry is a natural way for learning about and celebrating many cultures.

Searching for Poetry on the Internet

The Internet is a rich source for finding rhyming poems and songs and support for writing poems. Here are suggestions to guide your search.

Classic Poems

www.storyit.com/Classics/JustPoems/index.htm (This site provides a collection of classic poems for children to read, including poems by Emily Dickinson, Edward Lear, Albert Midlane, and others. Most of the poems are lightly illustrated and can be used to print individual student copies or post on bulletin or literature boards. The site also has writing prompts for stories and other activities based on themes, shapes, and alphabet.)

www.world-english.org/poetry.htm (another source for classic poems)

www.pitara.com/talespin/poems.asp (This site offers a large assortment of poems for children that includes "evergreen classics." You will also find new poems on different themes, including juvenile poetry about animals, parties, trees, and friendship. *Note*: There are quite a few advertisements on this site that you have to navigate.)

www.squidoo.com/classic-funny-poems-for-kids (This easy-to-navigate site features classic poems with amusing stories; poets include Longfellow, Lear, and Belloc among others.)

www.poemhunter.com/classics (This link takes you on a search for poets and their poems. *Note*: There were a few racy ads on this site. It is definitely for older readers; however, used judicially, it can be a useful site.)

www.everypoet.com/archive (This is a good archive of poems listed by poet. *Note*: There are a few annoying ads.)

Help With Writing Poems and Poems Written by Kids

www.kathimitchell.com/poemtypes.html (Easy to navigate, this site will be helpful to teachers who want to explore different types of poetry with their students; it features examples of how to do acrostic, alphabet, autobiographical, cinquain, and many other types of poems.)

www.gigglepoetry.com (On this site, you'll find lessons on how to write poetry, including "poems about me," family poems, animal poems, tall tales, school poems, silly rhymes, holiday themes, silly songs, and much more. This is a wonderful site, and many of the other sites have links to it. It is a great resource for teachers.)

mgfx.com/Kidlit/kids/artlit/poetry/index.htm (This site features kid-published poetry organized by age and provides some great examples of rhyming poetry and other poems published by children. It is also a nice resource for teachers who want to publish some of their students' poems.)

www.kidsturncentral.com/topics/hobbies/kidspoems.htm (This is another site that publishes kids' poetry.)

pbskids.org/arthur/games/poetry/what.html (On this PBS site, kids learn about different types of poems, including narrative, limericks, haiku, free verse, cinquains, and lyric poems. Students can also write their own poems.)

Songs

kids.niehs.nih.gov/musica.htm (This National Institute of Environmental Health Sciences Web site has some wonderful songs and sing-along activities arranged alphabetically and by theme. Many of the songs included here reinforce the word family-fluency connection.)

www.indianchild.com/nursery%20rhymes.htm (with sound) (Listen to musical nursery rhymes, such as "Baa Baa Black Sheep," "Hickory Dickory Dock," and others. The words/lyrics are included along with music.)

http://bussongs.com (This site has the largest collection of children's music on the Internet and contains lyrics, videos, and music for 2,108 kid's songs and nursery rhymes.)

judyanddavid.com/cma.html (This site has a children's music archive. It provides lyrics, sing-along suggestions, coloring sheets, and other activities.)

www.theteachersguide.com/ChildrensSongs.htm (At this site, the songs are arranged in alphabetical order and set up for easy browsing. If you are unsure about the title of a song, the site also includes a feature to help you search the lyrics and identify it.)

www.contemplator.com/america (You'll find popular songs in American history here. Many of the songs are from America's colonial and revolutionary era and originated in England, Scotland, and Ireland.)

www.scoutsongs.com/categories/patriotic.html (This site includes many scout songs and other patriotic music.)

Poems for Kids

www.poetry4kids.com/categories (Poems are arranged by category: animal antics, family food, food fun, holiday happenings. You can also rate the poems on this site. Many of the poems include rhyming patterns that can be used in the classroom.)

www.poetryarchive.org/childrensarchive/home.do (This archive contains different types of children's poetry about animals, clothes, dance, death, family, fathers, themes, forms, and poets. It allows you to search for poems or for poets and is easy to navigate.)

www.jeffspoemsforkids.com (Jeff Mondak's site starts out with a "poem of the week." It also includes information about the poet, as well as songs and lyrics written by Jeff Mondak. Many of the poems rhyme and can be used to create good word-family activities.)

www.funny-poems.co.uk (This site includes funny poetry arranged by themes and features poetry writing contests. *Note*: Spend some time examining this site before sending kids to it. Some of the poems are rude and crude, which is actually a theme! Most are harmless, but some may be inappropriate for young children.)

www.gardenofsong.com (This site includes different pages of poems written by different authors of all ages. There are categories, but they are somewhat random [stories of our lives]. The site also includes alphabet pages. *Note*: As the poems are by children of all ages, some are filled with teen angst. Examine the site before sending young children to it.)

www.helium.com/knowledge/127805-poetry-fantasy-poems-for-children (This site takes you directly to 44 fantasy poems in a list. *Note*: There are quite a few flashing advertisements on this site that are distracting.)

Poetry Resources for Teachers

www.apples4theteacher.com/poetry.html (This site breaks down printable poems by themes—animals, colors [nursery rhymes that use color words,] Earth Science, election day, family, friendship and more. This is a great site for teachers. *Note*: There are a few pop-ups, but other than that, it is easy to navigate and useful.)

www.poetryteachers.com (This site appears to be the same as the giggle poetry site [*www. gigglepoetry.com*] described earlier, but perhaps is organized a little differently for teachers. It contains the same pictures and links as the giggle site.)

www.kn.pacbell.com/wired/fil/pages/listpoetrymr14.html (This is a Web site with a variety of links concerning poetry, including Scholastic Web sites. It features different authors, writing activities, and Internet resources. *Note*: Some links were not active, and some parts were difficult to navigate; however, there were some great links. It was created by a school librarian.)

Word Families and Phonics Resources

www.kidzone.ws/phonics/activity1.htm (This site introduces the reader to word families and word-family activities. It has several other links that support word families and poetry.)

www.kidzone.ws/phonics/index.htm (This is another great link from kidzone.)

www.readwritethink.org/classroom-resources/student-interactives/word-family-sort-30052. html (This site, sponsored by IRA and NCTE, provides some great word family practice and support. It is easy to navigate and useful for teachers.)

www.mrsjonesroom.com/teachers/wordfamilies.html (This site has many terrific teacher resources related to phonics and fluency. It includes word-family activities, nursery rhymes, and other rhyming poetry. *Note*: Some of the links did not work, but overall, it is a very useful teacher resource).

www.readingrockets.org/article/13750 (This Reading Rockets page includes information about word families and shares ideas on how to teach them.)

www.enchantedlearning.com/rhymes/wordfamilies (This site includes many word family examples, along with a wealth of activities that can support teaching word families. It also includes poems and nursery rhymes organized by word families. A wonderful resource!)

Holiday Theme Poems

www.alphabet-soup.net/hall/hallo5.html (This link takes you directly to Halloween poems, and you can also submit your own. It is a fun site with great rhyming holiday theme poems.)

poetry.about.com/od/ourpoemcollections/a/christmaspoems.htm (There are a lot of poems related to Christmas at this site, and it includes the year each poem was written and the poet's name. Many include word families, making it a good resource for teachers.)

Nursery Rhymes

www.apples4theteacher.com/mother-goose-nursery-rhymes (These Mother Goose nursery rhymes are broken down into themes—color words, telling time, character sketches, days of the week, months of the year, riddles, and so on.)

kidsfront.com/rhymes-for-kids.html (The nursery rhymes on this site range from classical to contemporary. This is a useful resource and fairly easy to navigate. *Note*: There are a few distracting ads, but overall, it is a good resource for teachers.)

www.storyit.com/Classics/Nursery/index.htm (You'll find nursery rhymes and additional links here.)

www.zelo.com/family/nursery/index.asp (This straightforward, easy-to-navigate site features children's nursery rhymes and a list of links to access poems. *Note*: It contains a few pop-ups.)

www.love-poems.me.uk/a_childrens_nursery_rhymes_index.htm (The poems on this site are broken down into themes: religious, American poets, holiday poems, sad, funny, nature, English poets, inspirational, love, friendship, famous, children's poems, and so on. It also includes a link for poetry terms and information about writing and publishing poetry.)

www.rhymes.org.uk (This site features nursery rhymes as well as lyrics, origins, and history of the poems.)

www.mothergoose.com (In addition to Mother Goose rhymes, this site offers coloring pages and crafts, a preschool computer game, and links to each of the 362 Mother Goose rhymes—in alphabetical order.)

References

Adams, M. J. (1990). *Beginning to read: Thinking and learning about print.* Cambridge, MA: MIT Press.

Allington, R. L. (1983). Fluency: The neglected reading goal. *The Reading Teacher, 36,* 556–561.

Anderson, R., Hiebert, E., Scott, J., & Wilkinson, I. (1985). *Becoming a nation of readers: The report of the Commission on Reading.* Washington, DC: National Institute of Education.

Bear, D. R., Invernizzi, M., Templeton, S., & Johnston, F. (2007). *Words their way: Word study for phonics, vocabulary, and spelling instruction* (4th ed.). Upper Saddle River, NJ: Prentice-Hall.

Beck, I. (2005). *Making sense of phonics: The hows and whys.* New York: Guilford.

Biemiller, A. (2003). Vocabulary: Needed if more children are to read well. *Reading Psychology, 24,* 323–335.

Burkhardt, R. M. (2006). *Using poetry in the classroom: Engaging students in learning.* Lanham, MD: Rowman & Littlefield.

Chomsky, N. A. (1957). *Syntactic structures.* The Hague: Mouton.

Cunningham, P. M. (2004). *Phonics they use* (4th ed.). New York: Allyn & Bacon.

Cunningham, P. M. (2009). *Phonics they use: Words for reading and writing.* Boston: Allyn and Bacon.

Cunningham, P. M., & Cunningham, J. W. (1992). Making words: Enhancing the spelling-decoding connection. *The Reading Teacher, 46,* 106–115.

Drew, E., & Connor, G. (1961). *Discovering modern poetry.* New York: Holt, Rinehart & Winston.

Duke, N. K., Pressley, M., & Hilden, K. (2004). Difficulties in reading comprehension. In C. A. Stone, E. R. Silliman, B. J. Ehren, and K. Apel (Eds.), *Handbook of language and literacy: Development and disorders,* pp. 501–520. New York: Guilford.

Duthie, C., & Zimet, E. (1992). Poetry is like directions for your imagination. *The Reading Teacher, 46,* 14–24.

Ehri, L. C. (2005). Learning to read words: Theory, findings, and issues. *Scientific Studies of Reading, 9,* 167–188.

Elster, C. A., & Hanauer, D. I. (2002). Voicing texts, voices around texts: Reading poems in elementary school classrooms. *Research in the Teaching of English, 37,* 89–134.

Fox, B. (2007). *Word identification strategies: Building phonics into a classroom reading program* (4th ed.). New York: Prentice Hall.

Fry, E. (1998). The most common phonograms. *The Reading Teacher, 34,* 284–289.

Gamse, B. C., Bloom, H. S., Kemple, J. J., Jacob, R. T., Boulay, B., Bozzi, L., Caswell, L., Horst, M., Smith, W. C., St. Pierre, R. G., & Unlu, F. (2008). Reading First impact study: Interim report. Washington, DC: U. S. Department of Education.

Gaskins, I., W., Ehri, L. C., Cress, C. O., O'Hara, C., & Donnelly, K. (1996–1997). Procedures for word learning: Making discoveries about words. *The Reading Teacher, 50,* 312–327.

Godden, R. (1988). Shining Popocatepetl: Poetry for children. *The Horn Book, 64,* 305–414.

Graves, D. (1992). *Explore poetry.* Portsmouth, NH: Heinemann.

Graves, M. F. (2006). *The vocabulary book: Learning and instruction.* New York: Teachers College Press.

Gunning, T. (1995). Word building: A strategic approach to the teaching of phonics. *The Reading Teacher, 48,* 484–488.

Heilman, A. J., Blair, T. R., & Rupley, W. H. (2002). *Principles and practices of teaching reading* (10th ed.). Columbus, OH: Merrill.

Holdaway, D. (1979). *The foundations of literacy.* Auckland, New Zealand: Ashton Scholastic.

Keillor, G. (2004, October, 18). *The Writer's Almanac.* Retrieved April 22, 2007, from http://writersalmanac.publicradio.org/programs/2004/10/18/index.html.

Kuhn, M. R., & Stahl, S. A. (2000). *Fluency: A review of developmental and remedial practices* (CIERA Rep. No. 2-008). Ann Arbor, MI: Center for the Improvement of Early Reading Achievement.

LaBerge, D., & Samuels, S. A. (1974). Toward a theory of automatic information processing in reading. *Cognitive Psychology, 6,* 293–323.

Moustafa, M. (1997). *Beyond traditional phonics.* Portsmouth, NH: Heinemann.

National Reading Panel. (2000). Report of the National Reading Panel: Teaching children to read. Report of the subgroups. Washington, DC: U.S. Department of Health and Human Services, National Institutes of Health.

Nicholson, T., Lillas, C., & Rzoska, M. A. (1988). Have we been misled by miscues? *The Reading Teacher, 42,* 6–10.

Norton, D. E. (1999). *Through the eyes of a child* (5th ed.). Upper Saddle River, NJ: Prentice Hall.

Parr, M., & Campbell, T. (2006). Poets in practice. *The Reading Teacher, 60,* 36–46.

Perfect, K. (1999). Rhyme and reason: Poetry for the heart and head. *The Reading Teacher, 52,* 728–737.

Pikulski, J. J., & Chard, D. J. (2005). Fluency: Bridge between decoding and reading comprehension. *The Reading Teacher, 58*(6), 510–519.

Rasinski, T. (2005). *Daily word ladders: Grades 2–3.* New York: Scholastic.

Rasinski, T. (2005). *Daily word ladders: Grades 4–6.* New York: Scholastic.

Rasinski, T. (2008). *Daily word ladders: Grades 1–2.* New York: Scholastic.

Rasinski, T. V. (2010). *The fluent reader: Oral and silent reading strategies for building word recognition, fluency, and comprehension* (2nd ed.). New York: Scholastic.

Rasinski, T. V., & Hoffman, J. V. (2003). Theory and research into practice: Oral reading in the school literacy curriculum. *Reading Research Quarterly, 38*, 510–522.

Rasinski, T. V., & Padak, N. D. (2007). *From phonics to fluency: Effective teaching of decoding and reading fluency in the elementary school* (2nd ed.). New York: Longman.

Rasinski, T. V., Padak, N. D., Linek, W. L., & Sturtevant, E. (1994). Effects of fluency development on urban second-grade readers. *Journal of Educational Research, 87*, 158–165.

Rasinski, T., & Zutell, J. (2010). *Essential strategies for word study.* New York: Scholastic.

Rasinski, T. V., Reutzel, C. R., Chard, D., & Linan-Thompson, S. (in press). Reading fluency. In M. L. Kamil, P. D. Pearson, P. Afflerbach, & E. B. Moje (Eds.), *Handbook of reading research* (Vol. IV). New York: Routledge.

Rasinski, T., Rupley, W., & Nichols, W. D. (2009). Two essential ingredients: Phonics and fluency getting to know each other. *The Reading Teacher, 62*(3), 257–260.

Routman, R. (2001). Everyone succeeds with poetry writing. *Instructor, 111*(1), 26–31.

Rupley, W. H., Logan, J. W., & Nichols, W. D. (1999). The role of vocabulary in a balanced view of reading. *The Reading Teacher, 52*(4), 238–247.

Samuels, S. J. (1979). The method of repeated readings. *The Reading Teacher, 32*, 403–408.

Snow, C., Burns, M., & Griffin, P. (1998). *Preventing reading difficulties in young children.* Washington, DC: National Academy Press.

Stahl, S. A. (1992). Saying the "p" word: Nine guidelines for exemplary phonics instruction. *The Reading Teacher, 45*, 618–625.

Stanovich, K. E. (1980). Toward an interactive-compensatory model of individual differences in the development of reading fluency. *Reading Research Quarterly, 16*, 32–71.

Strickland, D., & Strickland, M. (1997). Language and literacy: The poetry connection. *Language Arts, 74*, 201–205.

Wilson, L. (1994). *Write me a poem: Reading, writing, and performing poetry.* Portsmouth, NH: Heinemann.